UNITED NATIONS CONFERENCE ON TRADE AND DEVELOPMENT

MODEL LAW ON COMPETITION

UNCTAD Series on Issues in Competition Law and Policy

Substantive Possible Elements for a competition law, commentaries
and alternative approaches in existing legislations

UNITED NATIONS
New York and Geneva, 2004

NOTE

The designations employed and the presentation of the material do not imply the expression of any opinion whatsoever on the part of the United Nations secretariat concerning the legal status of any country, territory, city or area, or of its authorities, or concerning the delimination of its frontiers or boundaries.

Material in this publication may be freely quoted or reprinted, but acknowledgement is requested, together with a reference to the documement number. A copy of the publication containing the quotation or reprint should be sent to the UNCTAD secretariat.

TD/RBP/CONF.5/7/Rev.2
UNITED NATIONS PUBLICATIONS
Sales. No. E.04.II.D.26
ISBN: 92-1-112633-9

CONTENTS

Introduction

(i)   The Intergovernmental Group of Expert Meeting on Competition Law and Policy, at its meeting held from 7 to 9 June 1999, agreed that UNCTAD should continue to publish as a non sessional document a revised version of the Commentary to the Model Law on Competition, taking into account new legislative developments in this field.

(ii) Accordingly, an Ad hoc Expert Group Meeting to revise the Model Law was held in Geneva on 19 February 2003. The present document contains a revised version of the draft possible elements for a competition law, as contained in Part I of the document "Draft commentaries to possible elements for a competition law of a Model Law or Laws" (TD/RBP/Conf.5/7), taking into account the comments received from member States either prior to the meeting or made during the discussions held during the Ad hoc Expert meeting mentioned above. The revisions to the Model Law on Competition, 2003 include only the changes relating to commentaries on Possible Elements of a Competition Law and to recent changes in national legislations. Suggestions made during the Ad hoc Expert Meeting for changes to the structure and the thrust of the Model Law requires substantive discussions and agreements on the proposed changes and therefore are not included in the current revision. The Intergovernmental Group of Experts on Competition Law and Policy scheduled for 2-4 July 2003 will have before it a summary of these proposals and a list of topics for its consideration and appropriate action.

PART I

Substantive Possible Elements for a Competition Law

<table>
</table>

CHAPTER I

Objectives or purpose of the law

To control or eliminate restrictive agreements or arrangements among enterprises, or mergers and acquisitions or abuse of dominant positions of market power, which limit access to markets or otherwise unduly restrain competition, adversely affecting domestic or international trade or economic development.

CHAPTER II

Definitions and scope of application

I. *Definitions*

(a) "Enterprises" means firms, partnerships, corporations, companies, associations and other juridical persons, irrespective of whether created or controlled by private persons or by the State, which engage in commercial activities, and includes their branches, subsidiaries, affiliates or other entities directly or indirectly controlled by them.

(b) "Dominant position of market power" refers to a situation where an enterprise, either by itself or acting together with a few other enterprises, is in a position to control the relevant market for a particular good or service or group of goods or services.

(c) "Mergers and acquisitions" refers to situations where there is a legal operation between two or more enterprises whereby firms legally unify ownership of assets formerly subject to separate control. Those situations include takeovers, concentrative joint ventures and other acquisitions of control such as interlocking directorates.

(d) "Relevant market" refers to the general conditions under which sellers and buyers exchange goods, and implies the definition of the boundaries that identify groups of sellers and of buyers of goods within which competition is likely to be restrained. It requires the delineation of the product and geographical lines within which specific groups of goods, buyers and sellers interact to establish price and output. It should include all reasonably substitutable products or services, and all nearby competitors, to which consumers could turn in the short term if the restraint or abuse increased prices by a not insignificant amount.

II. *Scope of application*

(a) Applies to all enterprises as defined above, in regard to all their commercial agreements, actions or transactions regarding goods, services or intellectual property.

(b) Applies to all natural persons who, acting in a private capacity as owner, manager or employee of an enterprise, authorize, engage in or aid the commission of restrictive practices prohibited by the law.

(c) Does not apply to the sovereign acts of the State itself, or to those of local governments, or to acts of enterprises or natural persons which are compelled or supervised by the State or by local governments or branches of government acting within their delegated power.

CHAPTER III

Restrictive agreements or arrangements

I. *Prohibition of the following agreements between rival or potentially rival firms, regardless of whether such agreements are written or oral, formal or informal:*

(a) Agreements fixing prices or other terms of sale, including in international trade;

(b) Collusive tendering;

(c) Market or customer allocation;

(d) Restraints on production or sale, including by quota;

(e) Concerted refusals to purchase;

(f) Concerted refusal to supply;

(g) Collective denial of access to an arrangement, or association, which is crucial to competition.

II. *Authorization or exemption*

Practices falling within paragraph I, when properly notified in advance, and when engaged in by firms subject to effective competition, may be authorized or exempted when competition officials conclude that the agreement as a whole will produce net public benefit.

CHAPTER IV

Acts or behaviour constituting an abuse of a dominant position of market power

I. *Prohibition of acts or behaviour involving an abuse, or acquisition and abuse, of a dominant position of market power*

A prohibition on acts or behaviour involving an abuse or acquisition and abuse of a dominant position of market power:

(i) Where an enterprise, either by itself or acting together with a few other enterprises, is in a position to control a relevant market for a particular good or service, or groups of goods or services;

(ii) Where the acts or behaviour of a dominant enterprise limit access to a relevant market or otherwise unduly restrain competition, having or being likely to have adverse effects on trade or economic development.

II. *Acts or behaviour considered as abusive:*

(a) Predatory behaviour towards competitors, such as using below cost pricing to eliminate competitors;

(b) Discriminatory (i.e. unjustifiably differentiated) pricing or terms or conditions in the supply or purchase of goods or services, including by means of the use of pricing policies in transactions between affiliated enterprises which overcharge or undercharge for goods or services purchased or supplied as compared with prices for similar or comparable transactions outside the affiliated enterprises;

(c) Fixing the prices at which goods sold can be resold, including those imported and exported;

(d) Restrictions on the importation of goods which have been legitimately marked abroad with a trademark identical with or similar to the trademark protected as to identical or similar goods in the importing country where the trademarks in question are of the same origin, i.e. belong to the same owner or are used by enterprises between which there is economic, organizational, managerial or legal interdependence, and where the purpose of such restrictions is to maintain artificially high prices;

(e) When not for ensuring the achievement of legitimate business purposes, such as quality, safety, adequate distribution or service:

(i) Partial or complete refusal to deal on an enterprise's customary commercial terms;

(ii) Making the supply of particular goods or services dependent upon the acceptance of restrictions on the distribution or manufacture of competing or other goods;

(iii) Imposing restrictions concerning where, or to whom, or in what form or quantities, goods supplied or other goods may be resold or exported;

(iv) Making the supply of particular goods or services dependent upon the purchase of other goods or services from the supplier or his designee.

III.   *Authorization or exemption*

Acts, practices or transactions not absolutely prohibited by the law may be authorized or exempted if they are notified, as described in article 7, before being put into effect, if all relevant facts are truthfully disclosed to competent authorities, if affected parties have an opportunity to be heard, and if it is then determined that the proposed conduct, as altered or regulated if necessary, will be consistent with the objectives of the law.

CHAPTER V

Notification

I.   *Notification by enterprises*

1.   When practices fall within the scope of articles 3 and 4 and are not prohibited outright, and hence the possibility exists for their authorization, enterprises could be required to notify the practices to the Administering Authority, providing full details as requested.

2.   Notification could be made to the Administering Authority by all the parties concerned, or by one or more of the parties acting on behalf of the others, or by any persons properly authorized to act on their behalf.

3.   It could be possible for a single agreement to be notified where an enterprise or person is party to restrictive agreements on the same terms with a number of different parties, provided that particulars are also given of all parties, or intended parties, to such agreements.

4.   Notification could be made to the Administering Authority where any agreement, arrangement or situation notified under the provisions of the law has been subject to change either in respect of its terms or in respect of the parties, or has been terminated (otherwise than by affluxion of time), or has been abandoned, or if there has been a substantial change in the situation (within (...) days/months of the event) (immediately).

5.   Enterprises could be allowed to seek authorization for agreements or arrangements falling within the scope of articles 3 and 4, and existing on the date of the coming into force of the law, with the proviso that they be notified within ((...) days/months) of such date.

6.   The coming into force of agreements notified could depend upon the granting of authorization, or upon expiry of the time period set for such authorization, or provisionally upon notification.

7.   All agreements or arrangements not notified could be made subject to the full sanctions of the law, rather than mere revision, if later discovered and deemed illegal.

II.   *Action by the Administering Authority*

1.   Decision by the Administering Authority (within (...) days/months of the receipt of full notification of all details), whether authorization is to be denied, granted or granted subject where appropriate to the fulfillment of conditions and obligations.

2.   Periodical review procedure for authorizations granted every (...) months/years, with the possibility of extension, suspension, or the subjecting of an extension to the fulfillment of conditions and obligations.

3.   The possibility of withdrawing an authorization could be provided, for instance, if it comes to the attention of the Administering Authority that:

(a) The circumstances justifying the granting of the authorization have ceased to exist;

(b) The enterprises have failed to meet the conditions and obligations stipulated for the granting of the authorization;

(c) Information provided in seeking the authorization was false or misleading.

CHAPTER VI

Notification, investigation and prohibition of mergers affecting concentrated markets

I.   *Notification*

Mergers, takeovers, joint ventures or other acquisitions of control, including interlocking directorships, whether of a horizontal, vertical, or conglomerate nature, should be notified when:

(i) At least one of the enterprises is established within the country; and

(ii) The resultant market share in the country, or any substantial part of it, relating to any product or service, is likely to create market power, especially in industries where there is a high degree of market concentration, where there are barriers to entry and where there is a lack of substitutes for a product supplied by firms whose conduct is under scrutiny.

II. *Prohibition*

Mergers, takeovers, joint ventures or other acquisitions of control, including interlocking directorships, whether of a horizontal, vertical or conglomerate nature, should be prohibited when:

(i) The proposed transaction substantially increases the ability to exercise market power (e.g. to give the ability to a firm or group of firms acting jointly to profitably maintain prices above competitive levels for a significant period of time); and

(ii) The resultant market share in the country, or any substantial part of it, relating to any product or service, will result in a dominant firm or in a significant reduction of competition in a market dominated by very few firms.

III. *Investigation procedures*

Provisions to allow investigation of mergers, takeovers, joint ventures or other acquisitions of control, including interlocking directorships, whether of a horizontal, vertical or conglomerate nature, which may harm competition could be set out in a regulation regarding concentrations.

In particular, no firm should, in the cases coming under the preceding subsections, effect a merger until the expiration of a (...) day waiting period from the date of the issuance of the receipt of the notification, unless the competition authority shortens the said period or extends it by an additional period of time not exceeding (...) days with the consent of the firms concerned, in accordance with the provisions of Possible Elements for Article 7 below. The authority could be empowered to demand documents and testimony from the parties and from enterprises in the affected relevant market or lines of commerce, with the parties losing additional time if their response is late.

If a full hearing before the competition authority or before a tribunal results in a finding against the transaction, acquisitions or mergers could be subject to being prevented or even undone whenever they are likely to lessen competition substantially in a line of commerce in the jurisdiction or in a significant part of the relevant market within the jurisdiction.

CHAPTER VII

The relationship between competition authority and regulatory bodies, including sectoral regulators

I. *Advocacy role of competition authorities with regard to regulation and regulatory reform*

An economic and administrative regulation issued by executive authorities, local self-government bodies or bodies enjoying a governmental delegation, especially when such a regulation relates to sectors operated by infrastructure industries, should be subjected to a transparent review process by competition authorities prior to its adoption. Such should in particular be the case if this regulation limits the independence and liberty of action of economic agents and/or if it creates discriminatory or, on the contrary, favourable conditions for the activity of particular firms – public or private – and/or if it results or may result in a restriction of competition and/or infringement of the interests of firms or citizens.

In particular, regulatory barriers to competition incorporated in the economic and administrative regulation, should be assessed by competition authorities from an economic perspective, including for general-interest reasons.

II. *Definition of regulation*

The term " regulation " refers to the various instruments by which Governments impose requirements on enterprises and citizens. It thus embraces laws, formal and informal orders, administrative guidance and subordinate rules issued by all levels of government, as well as rules issued by non-governmental or professional self-regulatory bodies to which Governments have delegated regulatory powers.

III. *Definition of regulatory barriers to competition*

As differentiated from structural and strategic barriers to entry, regulatory barriers to entry result from acts issued or acts performed by governmental executive authorities, by local self-government bodies, and by non-governmental or self-regulatory bodies to which Governments have delegated regulatory powers. They include administrative barriers to entry into a market, exclusive rights, certificates, licences and other permits for starting business operations.

IV. *Protection of general interest*

Irrespective of their nature and of their relation to the market, some service activities performed by private or government-owned firms can be considered by Governments to be of general interest. Accordingly, the providers of services of general interest can be subject to specific obligations, such as guaranteeing universal access to various types of quality services at affordable prices. These obligations, which belong to the area of social and economic regulation, should be set out in a transparent manner.

CHAPTER VIII

Some possible aspects of consumer protection

In a number of countries, consumer protection legislation is separate from restrictive business practices legislation.

CHAPTER IX

The Administering Authority and its organization

1. The establishment of the Administering Authority and its title.

2. Composition of the Authority, including its chairmanship and number of members, and the manner in which they are appointed, including the authority responsible for their appointment.

3. Qualifications of persons appointed.

4. The tenure of office of the chairman and members of the Authority, for a stated period, with or without the possibility of reappointment, and the manner of filling vacancies.

5. Removal of members of the Authority.

6. Possible immunity of members against prosecution or any claim relating to the performance of their duties or discharge of their functions.

7. The appointment of necessary staff.

CHAPTER X

Functions and powers of the Administering Authority

I. *The functions and powers of the Administering Authority could include (illustrative):*

(a) Making inquiries and investigations, including as a result of receipt of complaints;

(b) Taking the necessary decisions, including the imposition of sanctions, or recommending same to a responsible minister;

(c) Undertaking studies, publishing reports and providing information to the public;

(d) Issuing forms and maintaining a register, or registers, for notifications;

(e) Making and issuing regulations;

(f) Assisting in the preparation, amending or review of legislation on restrictive business practices, or on related areas of regulation and competition policy;

(g) Promoting exchange of information with other States.

II. *Confidentiality*

1. According information obtained from enterprises containing legitimate business secrets reasonable safeguards to protect its confidentiality.

2. Protecting the identity of persons who provide information to competition authorities and who need confidentiality to protect themselves against economic retaliation.

3.   Protecting the deliberations of government in regard to current or still uncompleted matters.

CHAPTER XI

Sanctions and relief

I.   *The imposition of sanctions, as appropriate, for:*

(i)   Violations of the law;

(ii)   Failure to comply with decisions or orders of the Administering Authority, or of the appropriate judicial authority;

(iii)   Failure to supply information or documents required within the time limits specified;

(iv)   Furnishing any information, or making any statement, which the enterprise knows, or has any reason to believe, to be false or misleading in any material sense.

II.   *Sanctions could include:*

(i)   Fines (in proportion to the secrecy, gravity and clear cut illegality of offences or in relation to the illicit gain achieved by the challenged activity);

(ii)   Imprisonment (in cases of major violations involving flagrant and intentional breach of the law, or of an enforcement decree, by a natural person);

(iii)   Interim orders or injunctions;

(iv)   Permanent or long term orders to cease and desist or to remedy a violation by positive conduct, public disclosure or apology, etc.;

(vi)   Divestiture (in regard to completed mergers or acquisitions), or rescission (in regard to certain mergers, acquisitions or restrictive contracts);

(vii)   Restitution to injured consumers;

(viii) Treatment of the administrative or judicial finding or illegality as prima facie evidence of liability in all damage actions by injured persons.

CHAPTER XII

Appeals

1.   Request for review by the Administering Authority of its decisions in the light of changed circumstances.

2.   Affording the possibility for any enterprise or individual to appeal within ( ) days to the (appropriate judicial authority) against the whole or any part of the decision of the Administering Authority, (or) on any substantive point of law.

CHAPTER XIII

Actions for damages

To afford a person, or the State on behalf of the person who, or an enterprise which, suffers loss or damages by an act or omission of any enterprise or individual in contravention of the provisions of the law, to be entitled to recover the amount of the loss or damage (including costs and interest) by legal action before the appropriate judicial authorities.

PART II

Commentaries on Chapters of the Model Law and alternative approaches in existing legislation

1. In line with the agreed conclusions of the Ad hoc Expert Meeting on the Revision of the Model Law on Competition held in Geneva on 19 February 2003, the secretariat has prepared revised commentaries to the draft possible elements and approaches in existing legislation for articles on a competition law as contained in Part I, taking into account recent International developments.

TITLE OF THE LAW:

Elimination or control of restrictive business practices:
Antimonopoly Law; Competition Act

COMMENTARIES ON THE TITLE OF THE LAW AND ALTERNATIVE APPROACHES IN EXISTING LEGISLATIONS

2. The draft possible elements for articles consider three alternatives for the title of the law, namely: "Elimination or Control of Restrictive Business Practices"[1], "Antimonopoly Law"[2] and "Competition Act"[3].

3. There is no common rule for the title of the competition laws. The different titles adopted generally reflect the objectives and hierarchy of the law, as well as the legal traditions of the countries concerned. Box 1 sets out the competition legislation adopted in most of the United Nations Member States, with its year of adoption. Examples of titles of the competition laws are given in annex 1 to the commentaries.

Box 1
Competition legislation in the United Nations Member States and other entities (with year of adoption)

Africa	Asia and Pacific	Countries in transition	Latin America and Caribbean	OECD countries
Algeria (1995)	China (1993) (Draft Revisión 2002/2003)	Armenia (2000)	Argentina (1980)	Australia (1974)
Benin				Austria (1988)
Botswana*		Azerbaijan**	Bolivia*	Belgium (1991)
Burkina Faso*	Fiji (1993)			Canada (1889)
Cameroon*		Belarus **	Brazil (rev. 1994, rev. 2002)	Czech Republic (1991, rev. 2001)
Central African Republic		Bulgaria (1991)		Denmark (1997, rev. 2002)
Côte d'Ivoire (1978)			Chile (1973, rev. 1980, rev. 2002)	European Union (1957)
Egypt*		Croatia (1995)		Finland (1992, rev. 2001)
Gabon (1998)	Indonesia (1999)		Colombia (1992)	France (1977, rev. 1986 et 2001)
Ghana*		Georgia**		
Kenya (1988) (Draft Revision 2002/2003)	India (1969, 2002)	Kazakhstan**	Costa Rica (1992)	Germany (1957, rev. 1998)
Lesotho*				Greece (1977, rev. 1995)
Malawi (1998)	Jordan*	Kyrgyzstan**	Dominican Republic*	Hungary (1996, rev 2000)
Mali (1998)		Lithuania (1992)	El Salvador*	Ireland (1991, rev. 1996, rev. 2002)
Mauritius*				
Morocco (1999)	Malaysia*	Mongolia (1993)	Guatemala*	Italy (1990)
Namibia (2003)				Japan (1947, rev. 1998)
Senegal (1994)	Pakistan (1970) (Draft Revision 2002)	Republic of Moldova**	Honduras*	Luxembourg (1970, rev. 1993)
Swaziland*				
South Africa (1955, amended 1979, 1998 & 2000)		Romania (1996)	Jamaica (1993)	Mexico (1992)
	Philippines*			Netherlands (1997)
Togo*		Russian Federation (1991)	Nicaragua*	New Zealand (1986)
Tunisia (1991)	Sri Lanka (1987)	Slovakia (1991)		Norway (1993)
			Panama (1996)	Poland (1990)
United Republic of Tanzania (1994),*** (Rev. 2002)		Slovenia (1991)		Portugal (1993)
Zambia (1994)	Taiwan Province of China (1992)	Tajikistan**	Paraguay*	Republic of Korea (1980, rev. 1999)
Zimbabwe (1996, rev 2001)			Peru (1990)	Spain (1989, rev. 1996)
		Turkmenistan**		Sweden (1993)
COMESA*	Thailand (1979 and 1999)			Switzerland (1985, rev. 1995)
UEMOA (1994, 2002)		Ukraine (2001)	Trinidad and Tobago*	Turkey (1994)
CARICOM*				United Kingdom (1890, rev.1973, 1980, 1998 & 2002)
MERCOSUR*	Viet Nam*	Uzbekistan	Venezuela (1991)	United States (1890, rev. 1976)

* Competition law in preparation.

** Most CIS countries have established an antimonopoly committee within the Ministry of Economy or Finance.

*** Fair Trade Practices Bureau established January 1999.

CHAPTER I

Objectives or purposes of the law

To control or eliminate restrictive agreements or arrangements among enterprises, or mergers and acquisitions or abuse of dominant positions of market power, which limit access to markets or otherwise unduly restrain competition, adversely affecting domestic or international trade or economic development.

COMMENTARIES ON CHAPTER I AND ALTERNATIVE APPROACHES IN EXISTING LEGISLATIONS

Objectives or purposes of the law

To control or eliminate restrictive agreements or arrangements among enterprises, or acquisition and/or abuse of dominant positions of market power, which limit access to markets or otherwise unduly restrain competition, adversely affecting domestic or international trade or economic development.

4. This article has been framed in accordance with section E, paragraph 2, of the Set of Principles and Rules, which sets out the primary principle on which States should base their restrictive business practices legislation. As in section A of the Set of Principles and Rules, States may wish to indicate other specific objectives of the law, such as the creation, encouragement and protection of competition; control of the concentration of capital and/or economic power; encouragement of innovation; protection and promotion of social welfare and in particular the interests of consumers, etc., and take into account the impact of restrictive business practices on their trade and development.

5. Approaches from various country legislation include, for example, the following objectives: in Algeria: "the organization and the promotion of free competition and the definition of the rules for its protection for the purpose of stimulating economic efficiency and the goodwill of consumers"[4]; in Armenia, the purpose of this Law is to "protect and promote economic competition, to ensure an appropriate environment for fair competition, the development of businesses and protection of consumer rights in the Republic of Armenia" (Art. 1, Law of the Republic of Armenia on Protection of Economic Competition); in Canada: "to maintain and encourage competition in order to promote the efficiency and adaptability of the Canadian economy, to expand opportunities for Canadian participation in world markets while at the same time recognizing the role of foreign competition in Canada, to ensure that the small and medium sized enterprises have an equitable opportunity to participate in the Canadian economy and to provide consumers with competitive prices and product choices"[5]; in Denmark, the purpose of the Act is "to promote efficient resource allocation by means of workable competition"; in Estonia the objective of the Estonian Competition Act is to safeguard competition in the interest of free enterprise upon the extraction of natural resources, manufacture of goods, provision of services and sale and purchase of products and services (hereinafter goods), and the preclusion and elimination of the prevention, limitation or restriction (hereinafter restriction) of competition in other economic activities (Article 1); in Gabon: "to ensure the freedom of prices and trade; to prevent any anti-competitive practice; to guarantee transparency in commercial transactions; to regulate economic concentration; to suppress hindrances to the free play of competition"[6]. In India, The Competition Act, 2002, objective is "keeping in view the economic development of the country,...to prevent practices having adverse effects on competition, to promote and sustain competition in markets, to protect the interests of consumers and to ensure freedom of trade carried on by other participants in markets, in India, and for matters connected therewith or incidental to"[7]; in Hungary: "the maintenance of competition in the market ensuring economic efficiency and social progress"[8]; in Mongolia: "to regulate relations connected with prohibiting and restricting state control over competition of economic entities in the market, monopoly and other activities impeding fair competition"[9]; in Norway: "to achieve efficiently utilization of society's resources by providing the necessary conditions for effective competition"[10]; in Panama: "to protect and guarantee the process of free economic competition and free concurrence, eliminating monopolistic practices and other restrictions in the efficient functioning of markets and services, and for safeguarding the superior interest of consumers"[11]; in Peru: "to eliminate monopolistic, controlist and restrictive practices affecting free competition, and procuring development of private initiative and the benefit of consumers"[12]; in the Russian Federation: "to prevent, limit and suppress monopolistic activity and unfair competition, and ensure conditions for the creation and efficient operation of commodity markets"[13]; in Spain the objectives of the law (Law 16/1989 on the Protection of Competition) are stressed in the "Statement of Purposes": competition, as the guiding

principle of any market economy, is an essential component of our society's model of economic organization and, in respect of individual liberties, constitutes the first and most important form in which the exercise of free enterprise is manifested. The protection of competition, therefore, in keeping with the requirements of the general economy and, where relevant, of planning, has to be conceived of as a mandate for the public authorities directly related to article 38 of the Constitution[14]; in Sweden: "to eliminate and counteract obstacles to effective competition in the field of production of and trade in goods, services and other products"[15]; in Switzerland: "to limit harmful consequences to the economic or social order imputable to cartels and other restraints on competition, and in consequence to promote competition in a market based on a liberal regime"[16]; in the United States: "a comprehensive charter of economic liberty aimed at preserving free and unfettered competition as the rule of trade. It rests on the premise that the unrestrained interaction of competitive forces will yield the best allocation of our economic resources, the lowest prices, the highest quality and the greatest material progress, while at the same time providing an environment conducive to the preservation of our democratic political and social institutions"[17]; in Taiwan province of China the legislative purpose of the Fair Trade Law is to maintain trading orders, to protect consumers' interests, to ensure fair competition, and to promote economic stability and prosperity[18]. In Tunisia, the purpose of the law is to define the provisions governing the freedom of prices, to establish the rules on free competition, to stipulate to this end the obligations incumbent on producers, traders, service providers and other intermediaries, and intended to prevent any anti-competitive practice, to ensure price transparency, and to curb restrictive practices and illicit price increases. Its purpose is also the control of economic concentration; in Ukraine the objective of the law is control of monopoly and prohibition of unfair competition entrepreneurial activities"; in Venezuela: "to promote and protect the exercise of free competition" as well as "efficiency that benefits the producers and consumers"[19]; the objectives in Zambian legislation are set in the preamble and are: to encourage competition in the economy by prohibiting anti-competitive trade practices; to regulate monopolies and concentrations of economic power; to protect consumer welfare; to strengthen the efficiency of production and distribution of services; to secure the best possible conditions for the freedom of trade; to expand the base of entrepreneurship; and to provide for matters connected with or incidental to the

foregoing. Under section 2 of the Act, "trade practice" means any practice related to the carrying on of any trade and includes anything done or proposed to be done by any person which affects or is likely to affect the method of trading of any trader or class of traders or the production, supply or price in the course of trade of any goods, whether real or personal, or of any service[20]; in the Andean Community, regulation refers to "the prevention and correction of distortions originated by business behaviours that impede, limit or falsify competition"[21]. In the European Community, the Treaty establishing the European Economic Community considers that "the institution of a system ensuring that competition in the common market is not distorted" constitutes one of the necessary means for promoting "a harmonious, balanced and sustainable development of economic activities" and "a high degree of competitiveness"[22]. A decision adopted by the Mercosur has as its objective "to assure equitable competition conditions within the economic agents from the Mercosur".

6. The texts proposed above refer to "control", which is in the title of the Set of Principles and Rules, and to "restrictive agreements and abuses of dominant positions of market power", which are the practices set out in sections C and D of the Set. The phrase "limit access to markets" refers to action designed to impede or prevent entry of actual or potential competitors. The term "unduly" implies that the effects of the restrictions must be perceptible, as well as unreasonable or serious, before the prohibition becomes applicable. This concept is present in the laws of many countries, such as Australia[23], Mexico[24], the Republic of Korea, the Russian Federation, the United Kingdom and the European Community.

7. In other legislation, certain cooperation agreements between small and medium size enterprises, where such arrangements are designed to promote the efficiency and competitiveness of such enterprises vis à vis large enterprises, can be authorized. This is the case in Germany and Japan. Also, in Japan enterprises falling in the small and medium size categories are defined on the basis of paid in capital and number of employees. In the United Kingdom, an agreement will not fall within Chapter I of the 1998 Competition Act, which prohibits agreements which prevent, restrict or distort competition and may affect trade within the United Kingdom, unless the effect on competition within the United Kingdom is "appreciable." As a general rule an agreement will not be deemed to have an "appreciable" effect where the

parties' combined market share of the relevant market does not exceed 25 per cent[25].

8. In the EU, it is up to member States to decide the manner in which any *de minimis* rule should be applied. There are essentially two alternatives. On the one hand, it can be left to the Administering Authority to decide on the basis of an evaluation of agreements or arrangements notified. In such case, the formulation of standards for exemption would be the responsibility of the Administering Authority. On the other hand, where the focus of the law is on considerations of "national interest", restrictions are examined primarily in the context of whether they have or are likely to have, on balance, adverse effects on overall economic development[26]. This concept, albeit with varying nuances and emphasis, has found expression in existing restrictive business practices legislation in both developed and developing countries[27]. Note, however, that the *de minimis* concept (i.e. that certain agreements are too small in size to do any real harm to competition and are not therefore of real concern to competition authorities) should be distinguished from the notion of certain agreements which have anti-competitive features and may nevertheless deserve to be exempted because of other redeeming features. Both concepts are recognised under both UK and EC law[28]. In the United States the jurisprudence takes a hard line against inclusion of non-competition issues as part of an antitrust analysis. For example, the United States Supreme Court stated that the purpose of antitrust analysis "is to form a judgment about the competitive significance of the restraint; it is not to decide whether a policy favoring competition is in the public interest, or in the interest of the members of an industry"[29].

CHAPTER II

Definitions and scope of application

I.   Definitions

(a) "Enterprises" means firms, partnerships, corporations, companies, associations and other juridical persons, irrespective of whether created or controlled by private persons or by the State, which engage in commercial activities, and includes their branches, subsidiaries, affiliates or other entities directly or indirectly controlled by them.

(b) "Dominant position of market power" refers to a situation where an enterprise, either by itself or acting together with a few other enterprises, is in a position to control the relevant market for a particular good or service or group of goods or services.

(c) "Mergers and acquisitions" refers to situations where there is a legal operation between two or more enterprises whereby firms legally unify ownership of assets formerly subject to separate control. Those situations include takeovers, concentrative joint ventures and other acquisitions of control such as interlocking directorates.

(d) "Relevant market" refers to the general conditions under which sellers and buyers exchange goods, and implies the definition of the boundaries that identify groups of sellers and of buyers of goods within which competition is likely to be restrained. It requires the delineation of the product and geographical lines within which specific groups of goods, buyers and sellers interact to establish price and output. It should include all reasonably substitutable products or services, and all nearby competitors, to which consumers could turn in the short term if the restraint or abuse increased prices by a not insignificant amount.

II.   Scope of application

(a) Applies to all enterprises as defined above, in regard to all their commercial agreements, actions or transactions regarding goods, services or intellectual property.

(b) Applies to all natural persons who, acting in a private capacity as owner, manager or employee of an enterprise, authorize, engage in or aid the commission of restrictive practices prohibited by the law.

(c) Does not apply to the sovereign acts of the State itself, or to those of local governments, or to acts of enterprises or natural persons which are compelled or supervised by the State or by local governments or branches of government acting within their delegated power.

COMMENTARIES ON CHAPTER II AND ALTERNATIVE APPROACHES IN EXISTING LEGISLATIONS

Definitions and scope of application

I.   *Definitions*

(a) "Enterprises" means firms, partnerships, corporations, companies, associations and other juridical persons, irrespective of whether created or controlled by private persons or by the State, which engage in commercial activities, and includes their branches, subsidiaries, affiliates or other entities directly or indirectly controlled by them.

9. The definition of "enterprises" is based on section B (i) (3) of the Set of Principles and Rules.

(b) "Dominant position of market power" refers to a situation where an enterprise, either by itself or acting together with a few other enterprises, is in a position to control the relevant market for a particular good or service or group of goods or services.

10. The definition of "dominant position of market power" is based on section B (i) (2) of the Set of Principles and Rules. For further comments on this issue, see paragraphs 55 to 60 below.

(d) "Relevant market" refers to the general conditions under which sellers and buyers exchange goods, and implies the definition of the boundaries that identify groups of sellers and of buyers of goods within which competition is likely to be restrained. It requires the delineation of the product and geographical lines within which specific groups of goods, buyers and sellers interact to establish price and output. It should include all reasonably substitutable products or services, and all nearby competitors, to which consumers could turn in the short term if the restraint or abuse increased prices by a not insignificant amount.

11. The definitions in the Set have been expanded to include one of "relevant market". The approach to this definition is that developed in the United States merger guidelines, which are generally accepted by antitrust economists in most countries[30].

12. Defining the "relevant market" is in simple terms identifying the particular product/services or class of products produced or services rendered by an enterprise(s) in a given geographic area. Box 2 provides

the basic reasoning regarding the relevant market and the market definition in competition law and policy. The United States Supreme Court has defined the relevant market as "the area of effective competition, within which the defendant operates."[31,32] Isolating the area of effective competition necessitates inquiry into both the relevant product market and the geographical market affected. It is also necessary to point out that defining the relevant market outlines the competitive situation the firm faces. Also, many jurisdictions, including the United Kingdom, allow for the possibility of taking into account supply side substitution when defining the relevant market. This is all the more important when the law involved implies actions which follow from market share alone. For example, some countries require "monopolies" (defined as firms having, say, a 30 or 40 per cent market share) to submit to price control and/or information provision. Indian Competition Act 2002 defines 'enterprise' as:

> "a person or a department of the Government, who or which is, or has been, engaged in any activity, relating to the production, storage, supply, distribution, acquisition or control of articles or goods, or the provision of services, of any kind, or in investment, or in the business of acquiring, holding, underwriting or dealing with shares, debentures or other securities of any other body corporate, either directly or through one or more of its units or divisions or subsidiaries, whether such unit or division or subsidiary is located at the same place where the enterprise is located or at a different place or at different places, but does not include any activity of the Government relatable to the sovereign functions of the Government including all activities carried on by departments of the Central Government dealing with atomic energy, currency, defence and space" (Sec. 2 (h))[33].

13. The product market (reference to product includes services) is the first element that must be taken into account for determining the relevant market. In practice, two closely related and complementary tests have been applied in the identification of the relevant product/ service market, namely the reasonable interchangeability of use and the cross elasticity of demand. In the application of the first criterion, two factors are generally taken into account, namely, whether or not the end use of the product and its substitutes are essentially the same, or whether the physical characteristics (or technical qualities) are similar enough to allow customers to switch easily from one to another. In the application of the cross elasticity test, the factor of price is central. It involves inquiry into the proportionate amount of increase in the

---

Box 2

Relevant market and market definition in competition law and policy

The relevant market, the place where supply and demand interact, constitutes a framework for analysis which highlights the competition constraints facing the firms concerned. The objective in defining the relevant market is to identify the firms that compete with each other in a given product and geographical area in order to determine whether other firms can effectively constrain the prices of the alleged monopolist. In other words, the task is to identify the competitors of these firms which are genuinely able to affect their behaviour and prevent them from acting independently of all real competitive pressure. Thus, definition of the relevant product and geographical markets is a key step in the analysis of many competition law cases.

The relevant product market is defined through the process of identifying the range of close substitutes for a product supplied by firms whose behaviour is under examination.

As globalization progresses, the relevant geographical market can be local, national, international or even global, depending on the particular product under examination, the nature of alternatives in the supply of the product, and the presence or absence of specific factors (e.g. transport costs, tariffs or other regulatory barriers and measures) that prevent imports from counteracting the exercise of market power domestically.

In the EU, for the definition of the relevant market, the competition authorities take account of a number of factors, such as the reactions of economic operators to relative price movements, the sociocultural characteristics of demand and the presence or absence of barriers to entry, such as transport costs. The same authorities tend to focus on demand trends in their analyses, and this impacts on the geographical dimension of the relevant market.

Sources: European Commission, OECD, UNCTAD and WTO.

---

quantities demand of one commodity as a result of a proportionate increase in the price of another commodity. In a highly cross elastic market a slight increase in the price of one product will prompt customers to switch to the other, thus indicating that the products in question compete in the same market while a low cross elasticity would indicate the contrary, i.e. that the products have separate markets.

In the Indian Competition Act, 2002, Section 2 (r, s, and t), relevant market is defined as follows:

(r) "relevant market" means the market which may be determined by the Commission with reference to the relevant product market or the relevant geographic market or with reference to both the markets;

(s) "relevant geographic market" means a market comprising the area in which the conditions of competition for supply of goods or provision of services or demand of goods or services are distinctly homogenous and can be distinguished from the conditions prevailing in the neighboring areas;

(t) "relevant product market" means a market comprising all those products or services which are regarded as inter changeable or substitutable by the consumer, by reason or characteristics of the products or services, their prices and intended use.

As regards "relevant product market", the Indian Competition Act considers the following factors:

(a) physical characteristics or end-use of goods;

(b) price of goods or services;

(c) consumer preferences;

(d) exclusion of in-house production;

(e) existence of specialized producers;

(f) classification of industrial products.

14. The geographical market is the second element that must be taken into account for determining the relevant market. It may be described broadly as the area in which sellers of a particular product or service operate. It can

also be defined as one in which sellers of a particular product or service can operate without serious hindrance[34]. The relevant geographical market may be limited for example, to a small city or it may be the whole international market. In between, it is possible to consider other alternatives, such as a number of cities, a province, a State, a region consisting of a number of States. For example in the context of controlling restrictive business practices in a regional economic grouping such as the European Community, the relevant geographical market is the "Common Market or a substantial part thereof". In this connection, the Court of Justice in the "European Sugar Industry" case[35] found that Belgium, Luxembourg, the Netherlands and the southern part of the then Federal Republic of Germany constituted each of them "substantial parts of the Common Market" (i.e. the relevant geographical market). Furthermore, the Court found that it was necessary to take into consideration, in particular, the pattern and volume of production and consumption of the product and the economic habits and possibilities open to sellers and buyers. For determining the geographical market, a demand oriented approach can also be applied. Through this approach, the relevant geographical market is the area in which the reasonable consumer or buyer usually covers his demand. For determining the "relevant geographic market", the Indian Competition Act, considers the following factors (Sec. 19 ((6)):

(a) regulatory trade barriers;

(b) local specification requirements;

(c) national procurement policies;

(d) adequate distribution facilities;

(e) transport costs;

(f) language;

(g) consumers preferences;

(h) need for secure or regular supplies or rapid after-sales services.

15. A number of factors are involved in determining the relevant geographical market including price disadvantages arising from transportation costs, degree of inconvenience in obtaining goods or services, choices available to consumers, and the functional level at which enterprises operate. In Chile the legislation does not

provide definitions of the concepts referred to above.

II.   *Scope of application*

(a) Applies to all enterprises as defined above, in regard to all their commercial agreements, actions or transactions regarding goods, services or intellectual property.

(b) Applies to all natural persons who, acting in a private capacity as owner, manager or employee of an enterprise, authorize, engage in or aid the commission of restrictive practices prohibited by the law.

(c) Does not apply to the sovereign acts of the State itself, or to those of local governments, or to acts of enterprises or natural persons which are compelled or supervised by the State or by local governments or branches of government acting within their delegated power.

Problems may arise when enterprises or natural persons belonging to the State or to local governments or when enterprises or natural persons which are compelled or supervised (i.e. regulated) in the name of the public interest by the State or by local governments or branches of government acting within their delegated power act beyond their delegated power. However, in some legislation, Acts of government officials or states owned enterprises which may lessen, eliminate or exclude competition in trade, commerce or industry are subject to competition law. Box 3 addresses the interaction of competition law and policy and regulation.

16. The scope of application takes into account section B (ii) of the Set. It has been expanded to clarify the application of the law to natural persons, but not to government officials acting for the Government. However, a natural person is not an "enterprise", unless incorporated as a "personal corporation". The model law could imply that an agreement between a Company and its own managing director is an agreement between two "enterprises" and thus a conspiracy. Legal analysis nearly everywhere concludes that this should not be the case. In Chile, however, "the person who executes or concludes, individually or collectively, any act is considered a personal corporation. (…)"[36]. In Colombia, article 25 of the Colombian Code of Commerce in this respect states: *"an enterprise shall be understood to mean any organized economic activity for the production, processing, distribution, administration or storage of goods, or for the supply of services. Such an activity shall be carried on by one or more*

Box 3

Competition law and policy and regulation

Basically, competition law and policy and regulation aim at defending the public interest against monopoly power. If both provide tools to a Government to fulfil this objective, they vary in scope and types of intervention. Competition law and regulation are not identical. There are four ways in which competition law and policy and regulatory problems can interact:

· *Regulation can contradict competition policy*. Regulations may have encouraged, or even required, conduct or conditions that would otherwise be in violation of the competition law. For example, regulations may have permitted price coordination, prevented advertising or required territorial market division. Other examples include laws banning sales below costs, which purport to promote competition but are often interpreted in anti competitive ways, and the very broad category of regulations that restrict competition more than necessary to achieve the regulatory goals. Modification or suppression of these regulations compels firms affected to change their habits and expectations.

· *Regulation can replace competition policy*. In natural monopolies, regulation may try to control market power directly, by setting prices (price caps) and controlling entry and access. Changes in technology and other institutions may lead to reconsideration of the basic premises in support of regulation, i.e. that competition policy and institutions would be inadequate to the task of preventing monopoly and the exercise of market power.

· *Regulation can reproduce competition law and policy*. Coordination and abuse in an industry may be prevented by regulation and regulators as competition law and policy do. For example, regulations may set standards of fair competition or tendering rules to ensure competitive bidding. However, different regulators may apply different standards, and changes or differences in regulatory institutions may reveal that seemingly duplicate policies may have led to different practical outcomes.

· *Regulation can use competition institutions' methods*. Instruments to achieve regulatory objectives can be designed to take advantage of market incentives and competitive dynamics. Coordination may be necessary in order to ensure that these instruments work as intended in the context of competition law requirements.

---

trade establishments". The EU approach to market definition is laid down in a Commission Notice on the definition of the relevant market for the purposes of Community Competition Law, OJ 1997 C 372, p. 5. See Box 2. Furthermore, natural persons may be classified as undertaking within the meaning of Articles 81 and 82 EC without being incorporated as a personal corporation if they are independent economic actors on markets for goods or services (see, for example, as regards Italian customs agents Case C-35/96 *Commission* v *Italy* [1998] ECR I-3851). The European Court of Justice has therefore classified on this basis lawyers, doctors and architects as undertakings within the meaning of Articles 81 and 82 EC. The definition of "enterprise" could be replaced by that of "economic agent", which would enable the Law to be applied also to natural persons who can act or, in fact, do act as professionals (lawyers, customs agents, etc.). In addition, falling within the scope of the Law would be certain types of legal persons who in principle are non-profit-making, such as associations or unions of enterprises and/or professionals, who may also engage in anti-competitive behaviours[37].

In Ukraine, an *economic entity* is defined as denoting such a legal person irrespective of its organisation and legal form, its form of ownership or such a natural person that is engaged in the production, sale or purchase of products and in other economic activities, including a person who exercises control over another legal or natural person; a group of economic entities if one or several of them exercise control over the others. Bodies of state power, bodies of local self-government, bodies of administrative and economic management and control shall also be considered as economic entities in terms of their activities in the production, sale, and purchase of products or in terms of their other economic activities[38]. In Armenia, the law states that "the present Law shall apply to those activities and conduct of economic entities, government and local government administration bodies, which might result in the restriction, prevention and distortion of competition or in acts of unfair competition, except where otherwise stipulated by law"[39].

In Korea, the scope of application of the MRFTA is extended to all enterprises. Exceptions extended to agriculture, fishery, forestry and mining, were abolished in the revision of the Law (Article 2-1). In the Ukraine, the law applies to relations involving economic entities (entrepreneurs), their associations, bodies of state power, citizens, legal persons and their associations not being economic entities (entrepreneurs) in conjunction with unfair competition, including acts made by them outside Ukraine, if these acts have negative effect on competition in its territory. In Zambia, Section 6(1) of the Zambian Act outlines the scope of application of the Act, presented as a function to monitor, control and prohibit acts or behavior which are likely to adversely affect competition and fair trading in Zambia. Acts or behaviour are carried out by "persons" who include an individual, a company, a partnership, an association and any group of persons acting in concert, whether or not incorporated, unlike in the model law. This covers both the public and private sectors, except for matters expressed in section 3[40].

17. Although virtually all international restrictive business practice codes, such as competition regulations of the European Community, the Andean Community Decision on Practices which Restrict Competition, and the MERCOSUR Decision on the Protection of Competition, apply only to enterprises, most national RBP laws apply to natural persons as well as to enterprises, since deterrence and relief can be more effective at the national level if owners or executives of enterprises can be held personally responsible for the violations they engage in or authorize. It is also important to mention that professional associations may also be considered as "enterprises", for the purposes of competition laws[41].

18. The scope of application has also been clarified to exclude the sovereign acts of local governments, to whom the power to regulate has been delegated, and to protect the acts of private persons when their conduct is compelled or supervised by Governments. It should be mentioned, however, that in section B (7) of the Set of Principles and Rules and in most countries having modern restrictive business practices legislation, the law covers State owned enterprises in the same way as private firms[42,43]. In Kenya, section 73 of the law applies to state corporations but provides also for exemptions under section 5 of the Kenyan Act[44].

19. The reference to intellectual property is consistent with virtually all antitrust laws, which treat licences of technology as "agreements" and scrutinize them for restrictions or abuses like any other agreement, except that the legal exclusivity granted by the State to inventors may justify some restrictions that would not be acceptable in other contexts.

20. It should be noted that in several countries, intellectual property[45] rights have given rise to competition problems. In view of the competition problems arising from the exercise of copyright, patents and trademark rights, several countries, such as Spain[46] and the United Kingdom[47], as well as the European Union, have considered it necessary to draw up specific regulations dealing with intellectual property rights in relation to competition. The United States has also adopted guidelines intended to assist those who need to predict whether the enforcement agencies will challenge a practice as anti competitive[48]. It is also important to take into account the provision for control of anti competitive practices in contractual licences included in the TRIPs Agreement[49]. In Chile, while article 5 states that, "without prejudice to what is established in the present law, the legal and regulatory provisions relating to intellectual and industrial property will continue in force (...)", the antimonopoly bodies take up such matters whenever they produce effects on competition[50].

CHAPTER III

Restrictive agreements or arrangements

I.   *Prohibition of the following agreements between rival or potentially rival firms, regardless of whether such agreements are written or oral, formal or informal:*

   (a) Agreements fixing prices or other terms of sale, including in international trade;

   (b) Collusive tendering;

   (c) Market or customer allocation;

   (d) Restraints on production or sale, including by quota;

   (e) Concerted refusals to purchase;

   (f) Concerted refusal to supply;

Box 4

Anti competitive practices likely to lead to an investigation

·   A secret cartel between competing firms governing prices or market shares;

·   A pricing regime pursued by a dominant firm not with the requirements of the market in mind, but with a view to driving a smaller competitor out of the market ("predatory pricing");

·   A dominant firm's refusal to supply;

·   A distribution system which rigidly divides the nationwide market into separate territories and which prevents parallel imports of the contract product.

(g) Collective denial of access to an arrangement, or association, which is crucial to competition.

II.   *Authorization or exemption*

Practices falling within paragraph I, when properly notified in advance, and when engaged in by firms subject to effective competition, may be authorized or exempted when competition officials conclude that the agreement as a whole will produce net public benefit.

COMMENTARIES ON CHAPTER III AND ALTERNATIVE APPROACHES IN EXISTING LEGISLATIONS

Restrictive agreements or arrangements

I.   *Prohibition of the following agreements between rival or potentially rival firms, regardless of whether such agreements are written or oral, formal or informal:*

(a) Agreements fixing prices or other terms of sale, including in international trade;

(b) Collusive tendering;

(c) Market or customer allocation;

(d) Restraints on production or sales, including by quota;

(e) Concerted refusals to purchase;

(f) Concerted refusal to supply;

(g) Collective denial of access to an arrangement, or association, which is crucial to competition.

21. The elements of this article are based upon section D, paragraph 3, of the Set of Principles and Rules and, as in the case of that paragraph, a prohibition in principle approach has been generally followed. Such an approach is embodied, or appears to be evolving, in the restrictive practice laws of many countries. See box 4 for most common anti competitive practices that are likely to lead to an investigation.

22. Agreements among enterprises are basically of two types, horizontal and vertical. Horizontal agreements are those concluded between enterprises engaged in broadly the same activities, i.e. between producers or between wholesalers or between retailers dealing in similar kinds of products. Vertical agreements are those between enterprises at different stages of the manufacturing and distribution process, for example, between manufacturers of components and manufacturers of products incorporating those goods, between producers and wholesalers, or between producers, wholesalers and retailers. Particular agreements can be both horizontal and vertical, as in price fixing agreements. Engaged in rival activities refers to competing enterprises at the horizontal level. Potentially rival activities refers to a situation where the other party or parties are capable and likely of engaging in the same kind of activity, for example, a distributor of components may also be a producer of other components.

23. Agreements among enterprises are prohibited in principle in the Set, "except when dealing with each other in the context of an economic entity wherein they are under common control, including through ownership, or otherwise not able to act independently of each other" (section D.3). It should be noted that a prevailing number of jurisdictions have ruled that firms under common ownership or control are not rival or potentially rival firms. In the United States, while some lower courts had this

rule to include companies which are majority owned by another firm[51], the Supreme Court has gone no further than deciding that a parent and its wholly owned subsidiary are incapable of conspiring for purposes of the Sherman Act[52].

24. Agreements or arrangements, whether they are written or oral, formal or informal, would be covered by the prohibition. This includes any agreement, whether or not it was intended to be legally binding. In this context, the Indian Competiton Act 2002 prohibits any agreement in respect of production, supply, distribution, storage or control of goods or provision of services, which cause or is likely to cause an appreciable adverse effect on competition within India. In the case of the following agreements there is a presumption of 'appreciable adverse effect on competition' within India, viz. horizontal agreements. The legislation of Pakistan defines an agreement as including "any arrangement or understanding, whether or not in writing, and whether or not it is or is intended to be legally enforceable"[53]. A similar definition is to be found in Algeria[54], Gabon, India and South Africa[55]. The legislation in Poland[56] and the Russian Federation[57] refers to "agreements in any form". The Law of Spain which is inspired by the European Community rules, has a generous wording covering multiple possibilities that go beyond agreements, namely "collective decisions or recommendations, or concerted or consciously parallel practices". A similar approach is followed by Côte d'Ivoire, Hungary, Peru and Venezuela[58], as well as by the Andean Community and MERCOSUR legislation.

25. Where arrangements are in writing, there can be no legal controversy as to their existence, although there might be controversy about their meaning. However, enterprises frequently refrain from entering into written agreements, particularly where it is prohibited by law. Informal or oral agreements raise the problem of proof, since it has to be established that some form of communication or shared knowledge of business decisions has taken place among enterprises, leading to concerted action or parallelism of behaviour on their part. In consequence, proof of concerted action in such instances is based on circumstantial evidence. Parallelism of action is a strong indication of such behaviour, but might not be regarded as conclusive evidence. An additional and important way for proving the existence of an oral agreement, far superior to evidence of parallel behaviour, is by direct testimony of witnesses.

26. Establishing whether parallel behaviour is a result of independent business decisions or tacit agreement would probably necessitate an inquiry into the market structure, price differentials in relation to production costs, timing of decisions and other indications of uniformity of enterprises behaviour in a particular product market. A parallel fall in prices can be evidence of healthy competition, while parallel increases should amount to evidence of tacit or other agreement or arrangement sufficient to shift the evidential burden to the enterprise or enterprises involved, which ought in turn to produce some evidence to the contrary as a matter of common prudence[59]. Another way in which competitive but parallel conduct might be distinguished from conduct that is the result of an anti competitive agreement is to inquire whether the conduct of a particular firm would be in its own interest in the absence of an assurance that its competitors would act similarly. Nevertheless, it is also important to mention that parallel price increases, particularly during periods of general inflation are as consistent with competition as with collusion and provide no strong evidence of anti competitive behaviour.

27. The restrictive business practices listed in (a) to (g) of article 3 are given by way of example and should not be seen as an exhaustive list of practices to be prohibited. Although the listing comprises the most common cases of restrictive practices, it can be expanded to other possibilities and become illustrative by introducing between the terms "prohibition" and "of the following agreements" the expressions "among other possibilities", "in particular", such as for example in Hungary[60], or "among others", such as for example in the Colombian legislation[61,62]; or by adding "other cases with an equivalent effect", as is done in the Andean Community Regulation[63]. By doing so, article 3 becomes a "general clause" that covers not only those agreements listed under (a) to (g) but also others not expressly mentioned which the Administrative Authority might consider restrictive as well.

28. Furthermore, in some countries, such as in India, certain agreements are evaluated by the Competition Commission of India based on their appreciable adverse effect on competition within India, based on rule of reason approach. These agreements include;

(i) "tie-in agreements";

(ii) exclusive supply agreements;

(iii) exclusive distribution agreements;

(iv) refusal to deal; and

(v) resale price maintenance.

29. A distinctive feature of the United States legislation developed in the application of Section 1 of the Sherman Act is the "per se" approach. While the guiding principle for judging anti competitive behaviour is the "rule of reason" (unreasonable restraint being the target of control determined on the basis of inquiry into the purpose and effects of an alleged restraint), the Supreme Court has held that "there are certain agreements or practices which, because of their pernicious effect on competition and lack of any redeeming virtue, are conclusively presumed to be unreasonable and therefore illegal without elaborate inquiry as to the precise harm they have caused or the business excuse for their use"[64]. Restrictions considered "per se" violations generally include price fixing, horizontal division of markets and consumers, and bid rigging.

30. It is to be noted that the European Community also considers a priori that agreements between undertakings (or concerted practices or decisions by associations of undertakings) that restrict competition are (due to the effect they may have in trade between member States) prohibited (article 81 (1) of the Treaty of Rome) and automatically void "nuls de plein droit" (article 81 (2) of the Treaty of Rome). It also considers that, under certain circumstances, those agreements could be exempted from the prohibition of article 81 (1), if they fulfil the following conditions (article 81 (3) of the Treaty of Rome):

(a) Contribute to improving the production or distribution of goods or to promote technical or economic progress;

(b) Allow the consumers a fair share of the resulting benefit;

(c) Do not impose on the undertakings concerned restrictions (on competition) which are not indispensable to the attainment of these objectives; and

(d) Do not afford such undertakings the possibility of eliminating competition in respect of a substantial part of the products in question.

A special feature of Russian legislation is the Absence of a "per se" approach in the ban on agreements; in other words, the antimonopoly authorities in the Russian Federation may prohibit agreements if they determine that such agreements have or may have the result of substantially restricting competition.

31. The Australian legislation prohibits most price fixing agreements, boycotts and some forms of exclusive dealing. Moreover, this is also the case of India, where, under the Monopolies and Restrictive Trade Practices Act, the term or condition of a contract for the sale of goods or any agreement which provides for minimum prices to be charged on the resale of goods are prohibited per se[65].

(a) Agreements fixing prices or other terms of sale, including in international trade;

32. The Set of Principles and Rules, in paragraph D.3 (a) calls for the prohibition of "agreements fixing prices, including as to exports and imports".

33. Price fixing is among the most common forms of restrictive business practices and, irrespective of whether it involves goods or services, is considered as per se violation in many countries[66]. In the United States, the Supreme Court limited the per se prohibition against resale price maintenance to minimum resale price maintenance, providing that maximum resale price maintenance is to be reviewed under a "rule of reason" analysis because it may lead to lower prices. Price fixing can occur at any level in the production and distribution process. It may involve agreements as to prices of primary goods, intermediary inputs or finished products. It may also involve agreements relating to specific forms of price computation, including the granting of discounts and rebates, drawing up of price lists and variations therefrom, and exchange of price information.

34. Price fixing may be engaged in by enterprises as an isolated practice or it may be part of a larger collusive agreement among enterprises regulating most of the trading activities of members, involving for example collusive tendering, market and customer allocation agreements, sales and production quotas, etc. Also, agreements fixing prices or other terms of sales prohibited under this paragraph may include those relating to the demand side, such as is the case of cartels aimed at or having the effect of enforcing buying power.

35. Concerning international trade, it is worth pointing out

that while price fixing with respect to goods and services sold domestically has been subject to strict control, under restrictive business practices legislation price fixing with respect to exports has, by and large, been permitted on the grounds that such activities do not affect the domestic market. In some countries the legislation specifically exempts export cartels on condition that they are notified and registered and that they do not adversely affect the domestic market. This is the case, for example, in Peru, and the United States. Participation of national industries in international cartels is prohibited by the legislation of the United States and other countries[67,68].

(b) Collusive tendering[69];

36. Collusive tendering is inherently anti competitive, since it contravenes the very purpose of inviting tenders, which is to procure goods or services on the most favourable prices and conditions. Collusive tendering may take different forms, namely: agreements to submit identical bids, agreements as to who shall submit the lowest bid, agreements for the submission of cover bids (voluntary inflated bids), agreements not to bid against each other, agreements on common norms to calculate prices or terms on bids, agreements to "squeeze out" outside bidders, agreements designating bid winners in advance on a rotational basis, or on a geographical or customer allocation basis. Such agreements may provide for a system of compensation to unsuccessful bidders based on a certain percentage of profits of successful bidders to divide among unsuccessful bidders at the end of a certain period.

37. Collusive tendering is illegal in most countries. Even countries that do not have specific restrictive business practices laws often have special legislation on tenders. Most countries treat collusive tendering more severely than other horizontal agreements, because of its fraudulent aspects and particularly its adverse effects on government purchases and public spending. In the People's Republic of China, the bid will be declared null and void and, according to circumstances, a fine will be imposed. In Kenya, for example, collusive tendering is considered a criminal offence punishable by up to three years' imprisonment where two or more persons tender for the supply or purchase of goods or services at a price, or on terms, agreed or arranged between them, except for joint tenders disclosed to, and acceptable to, the persons inviting the tender. In Sweden, there are no special provisions concerning collusive tendering in the Competition Act. This kind of horizontal cooperation falls under the general prohibition of anti competitive agreements or concerted practices.

(c) Market or customer allocation;

38. Customer and market allocation arrangements among enterprises involve the assignment to particular enterprises of particular customers or markets for the products or services in question. Such arrangements are designed in particular to strengthen or maintain particular trading patterns by competitors forgoing competition in respect of each other's customers or markets. Such arrangements can be restrictive to a particular line of products, or to a particular type of customer.

39. Customer allocation arrangements occur both in domestic and international trade; in the latter case they frequently involve international market divisions on a geographical basis, reflecting previously established supplier buyer relationships. Enterprises engaging in such agreements virtually always agree not to compete in each other's home market. In addition, market allocation arrangements can be designed specifically for this purpose.

(d) Restraints on production or sales, including by quota;

40. Market sharing arrangements may also be devised on the basis of quantity allocations rather than on the basis of territories or customers. Such restrictions are often applied in sectors where there is surplus capacity or where the object is to raise prices. Under such schemes, enterprises frequently agree to limit supplies to a proportion of their previous sales, and in order to enforce this, a pooling arrangement is often created whereby enterprises selling in excess of their quota are required to make payments to the pool in order to compensate those selling below their quotas.

(e) Concerted refusals to purchase;

(f) Concerted refusal to supply;

41. Concerted refusals to purchase or to supply, or the threat thereof, are one of the most common means employed to coerce those who are not members of a group to follow a prescribed course of action. Group boycotts may be horizontal (i.e. cartel members may agree among themselves not to sell to or buy from certain customers), or vertical (involving agreements between parties at different levels of the production and

---

Box 5

Vertical restraints and competition law and policy

The concept of vertical restraints refers to certain types of business practices that relate to the resale of products by manufacturers or suppliers and are thus embodied in agreements between operators on a line of business situated at different stages of the value added chain. They include resale price maintenance (RPM), exclusive dealing and exclusive territory or territorial (geographical) market restrictions on distributors. While the first has remained highly controversial among economists, exclusivity practices raise fewer concerns.

·   RPM. This is basically found in an agreement among retailers, enforced by the producers, not to compete on prices (thereby creating a "network"). Generally RPM refers to the setting of *retail* prices by the original manufacturer or supplier. It is often called by the euphemism "fair trade" in North America or Europe. In some cases, a supplier can exercise control over the product market. In concentrated markets (e.g. where there are few "networks" offering the same type of goods of different brands) or when market power exists (i.e. where inter brand competition is absent, as is frequently the case in developing countries), competition authorities should request detailed justifications, on efficiency grounds, by producers willing to fix retail prices or should seek to remove any regulatory barriers inhibiting entry by new operators. RPM is an area where competition policies in mature and competitive markets and developing markets may differ sharply.

·   Exclusive dealing. This is found in an agreement between a manufacturer who offers a sales contract conditional on the buyer's accepting not to deal in the goods of a competitor. The restriction is placed on the firm's choice of buyers or suppliers.

·   Exclusive territory or territorial market restrictions. This is found in an agreement by which a manufacturer restricts the retailers to competing on the distribution of its products.

·   Tying arrangements. These are agreements by which a manufacturer restricts the source of supplies for particular inputs used by retailers. Under U.S. Law, a tying arrangement is defined as "an agreement by a party to sell one product but only on condition that the buyer also purchases a different (or tied) product, not purchase the product from any other supplier".

In many jurisdictions, vertical restraints are subject to a "rule of reason" approach, which reflects the fact that such restraints are not always harmful and may, actually, be beneficial in particular market structure circumstances. Non price vertical restraints are rarely opposed by competition authorities.

---

distribution stages refusing to deal with a third party, normally a competitor to one of the above). For a brief review of the treatment of vertical restraints by competition law and policy see box 5. Vertical restraints can also be considered in relationship to the position of a firm on the market.

42. Boycotts are considered illegal in a number of countries, particularly when they are designed to enforce other arrangements, such as collective resale price maintenance and collective exclusive dealing arrangements. For example, boycotts or stop lists for collective enforcement of conditions as to resale price maintenance are prohibited in the United Kingdom.

In the United States, the Supreme Court held in Northwest Wholesale Stationers, Inc. v. Pacific Stationery & Printing Co., 472 U.S. 284 (1985), that not all concerted horizontal refusals to deal warrant per se treatment. The defendant, a purchasing cooperative, had expelled a member without providing either an explanation at that time or a procedural means to challenge the expulsion. The Court found that such cooperatives typically are designed to increase economic efficiency and held that unless the cooperative possessed market power or exclusive access to an "element essential to effective competition," the expulsion of the member should be judged under the rule of reason and therefore might well be lawful. In contrast, in FTC v. Superior Court Trials Lawyers Ass'n, 493 U.S. 411

(1990), the Supreme Court held that a group boycott designed to affect the price paid for the services of the group's members was per se unlawful without regard to the market power of the participants.

43. Concerted refusals to supply, whether it be to a domestic buyer or an importer, are also a refusal to deal. Refusals to supply potential importers are usually the result of customer allocation arrangements whereby suppliers agree not to supply other than designated buyers. They can also be a result of collective vertical arrangements between buyers and sellers, including importers and exporters.

44. The European Commission has developed a systematic policy concerning "parallel" imports or exports. Among others, it considers that, although existing exclusive distribution agreements (which could be accepted due to rationalization), parallel trade must be always authorized because it constitutes the only guarantee against member States' market compartmentalization, and the application of discriminatory policies concerning prices. The exemption rules on exclusive agreements contained in Commission Regulation No. 1983/83 explicitly prohibits all restrictions on parallel imports and also includes a provision stating that every exclusive dealer is responsible for losses coming from a client outside its territory[70].

(g) Collective denial of access to an arrangement, or association, which is crucial to competition.

45. Membership of professional and commercial associations is common in the production and sale of goods and services. Such associations usually have certain rules of admittance and under normal circumstances those who meet such requirements are allowed access. However, admittance rules can be drawn up in such a manner as to exclude certain potential competitors either by discriminating against them or acting as a "closed shop"[71]. Nevertheless, as ruled in the United States, valid professional concerns can justify exclusions of individuals from professional associations[72].

46. Collective denial of access to an arrangement may also take the form of denying access to a facility that is necessary in order to compete effectively in the market[73].

II.   *Authorization or exemption*

Practices falling within paragraph I, when properly notified

in advance, and when made by firms subject to effective competition, may be authorized when competition officials conclude that the agreement as a whole will produce net public benefit.

47. Paragraph II of proposed article 3 deals with authorization, which is the way to vest national authorities with discretionary powers to assess national interests vis à vis the effects of certain practices on trade or economic development. Enterprises intending to enter into restrictive agreements or arrangements of the type falling under paragraph I would accordingly need to notify the national authority of all the relevant facts of the agreement in order to obtain authorization in accordance with the procedure described in article 6. It is to be noted that the policy whereby competition agencies may authorize firms to engage in certain conduct if the agency determines that such practices produce a "net public benefit" is opposed to one in which agencies authorize practices that "do not produce public harm". Proving that the practice produces "net public benefit" may well place an unjustified burden of proof on firms and result in the prohibition of pro competitive practices[74]. Whatever the approach followed in a particular legislation ("produce net public benefit" or "do not produce public harm"), authorization procedures must be characterized by transparency.

48. As an example, in the European Community, article 81 (1) of the Treaty of Rome prohibits and declares "incompatible with the common market: all arrangements between undertakings, decisions by associations of undertakings and concerted practices which may affect trade between Member States and which have as their object or effect the prevention, restriction or distortion of competition within the common market". However the prohibition is not absolute, since article 81 (3) declares that the provisions of paragraph (1) may be declared inapplicable if such agreements or decisions contribute to "improving the production or distribution of goods or to promoting technical or economic progress, while allowing consumers a fair share of the resulting benefit", with the provision that they do not:

(a) Impose on the undertakings concerned restrictions which are not indispensable to the attainment of these objectives;

(b) Afford such undertakings the possibility of eliminating competition in respect of a substantial part of the products in question.

49. The European Commission and the Court of Justice of the European Communities are nevertheless generally reticent to authorize agreements that fall within the categories considered within article 81 (1) of the Treaty of Rome. This is specially true concerning market allocation and price fixing[75].

50. Many laws, such as those of Germany, Italy, Japan, Spain, Sweden and, Venezuela, to cite some examples, provide for possibilities of authorization under particular circumstances, and for a limited period of time, such as crisis cartels (referred to as depression cartels in Japan and Spain), and rationalization cartels[76]. However, there are certain exceptions, since while the law does not allow the concession of any monopoly for exercising economic activities, such as extractive, industrial, commercial or services activities, to be granted to private individuals, it does provide for the possibility that the monopoly of such activities will be reserved, only by means of law, to certain institutions. The other exception is based on "national interest", i.e. the execution and maintenance of those acts or contracts referred to in the foregoing articles can be authorized by a supreme decree founded upon a previous favourable report of the Resolutive Commission (Competition Tribunal) and providing that they are necessary for the stability or development of national investments and consist in acts or contracts to which any of the institutions referred to in article 4 (2) is a party. The Colombian legislation lists research and development agreements, compliance with standards and measures legislation, and procedures, methods and systems for the use of common facilities[77]. In Italy, the Competiton Authority may authorize, for a limited period, agreements or categories of agreements prohibited under the section Agreements Restricting Freedom of Competition, which have the effect of improving the conditions of supply in the market, leading to substantial benefits for consumers. Such improvements shall be identified taking also into account the need to guarantee the undertakings the necessary level of international competitiveness and shall be related, in particular with increases of production, improvements in the quality of production or distribution, or with technical and technological progress". The Hungarian legislation exempts agreements that contribute to a more reasonable organization of production or distribution, the promotion of technical or economic progress, or the improvement of competitiveness or of the protection of the environment; provided that they allow consumers a fair share of the resulting benefit; that their restrictive effects do not exceed the extent necessary to attain economically justified common goals; and that they do not create the possibility of excluding competition in respect of a substantial part of the products concerned[78]. The Indian Competition Act 2002 authorizes the Central Government to exempt, by notification, from the application of the Act, or any provision thereof, and for such period as it may specify in such notification, any class of enterprises, in the interest of security of the State or public interest; any practice or agreement arising out of and in accordance with any obligation assumed by India under any treaty, agreement or convention with any other country or countries; and any enterprise which performs a sovereign function on behalf of the central Government or a State Government, provided that in case an enterprise is engaged in any activity including the activity relatable to the sovereign function of the Government, the Central Government may grant exemption only in respect of activity relatable to the sovereign functions (Sec. 54 of the Act). The new Lithuanian law exempts agreements that promote investment, technical or economic progress or improve the distribution of goods, thus allowing all consumers to get additional benefit, also when the agreement does not impose restrictions on the activity of the parties thereto which are not indispensable to the attainment of the objectives referred to and the agreement does not afford contracting parties the possibility to restrict competition in a large relevant market share[79].

In the Russian Federation, such agreements are lawful if they show that the positive effect of their actions, including in the socio economic sphere, will exceed the negative effects for the market goods under consideration[80]. The law of Slovakia contains provisions which allow automatic exemption from the ban on restrictive agreements. In this country, if restrictive agreements or arrangements comply with the criteria specified in the law, no ban on these agreements can be applied. Notification of the agreements is not required by law. There is a legal presumption that restrictive agreements are prohibited unless the parties to the agreement prove that criteria set out by the law are fulfilled. In the Slovak Republic, agreements restricting competition are banned but the competition Office may decide that the ban should not apply to a certain agreement, if such an agreement meets the terms determined by the Act. Thus, an automatic exemption from the ban on restrictive agreements is not possible, and only the Office may grant an individual exemption for certain agreements restricting competition, if such an agreement meets particular terms defined in the Act. In June 2002, a new Act No. 465/2002 which introduces block exemptions for some groups of agreements has been adopted as an ammendent to the Slovak competition law[81]. For examples of agreements that can escape competition law prohibitions, see box 6. For examples of agreements that require individual exemptions to escape the prohibition of competition laws, see box 7.

51. Furthermore, certain sectors of the economy may be exempted from the application of the law, such as banking, and public services including transport and communications, the provision of water, gas, electricity and fuel, because those activities are regulated by other

---

Box 6

Some agreements can escape competition law prohibitions

These agreements can be explicitly exempted by laws, regulations or "rule of reason" reasoning because they contribute to economic development and market efficiency. Within the EU, most of these agreements are "category exemption".

· Exclusive distribution agreements;

· Exclusive purchasing agreements;

· Patent licensing agreements;

· Motor car distribution and servicing agreements;

· Specialization agreements;

· Research and development cooperation agreements;

· Franchise agreements;

· Technology transfer agreements;

· Certain types of agreements in the insurance sector.

Sources: OECD and European Commission.

Box 7

Agreements requiring individual exemption

Some agreements must be considered in connection with market structure criteria. As such, these agreements require individual exemption by administrative decision after applying "rule of reason" reasoning. They are the following:

· Most types of joint venture agreements which do not fall under the research and development block exemption and which do not amount to mergers;

· Most exclusive licences of industrial property which do not fall within the technology transfer block exemptions;

· Restructuring agreements or "crisis cartels";

· Agreements establishing joint sales or buying agencies;

· Information agreements;

· Agreements establishing the rules of a trade association;

· Agreements or decisions establishing trade fairs.

laws or regulatory agencies. In other words, specific legislation creates the exemption. Such sectoral exceptions could be covered by an exemption clause under the scope of application. In recent years, however, with the rising trend of "deregulation", many countries have amended their legislation to include previously exempted sectors in the purview of the law. In the United Kingdom, for example, even State owned utilities are covered by competition law and regularly subject to investigation. The same occurs in the European Commission which, since 30 years now, includes within its competition rules State owned enterprises and State monopolies having a commercial character. For a presentation of the interaction between competition law and regulation, see box 3 above.

52. It should be noted that laws adopting the per se prohibition approach as generally do those of the United States do not envisage any possibility of exemption or authorization, and therefore do not have a notification system for horizontal restrictive business practices. Regarding the use of the per se approach in the United States, it is limited to a narrow category of restrictive business practices considered "naked" restraints, or those restraints that are not reasonably related to a firm's business operations. Even horizontal agreements on price may be deemed "non-naked," and subject to a "rule of reason" analysis, if based on an efficiency enhancing or pro-competitive rationale, *e.g.,* the restraint is necessary to secure the production of a new good[82]. While the United States law does not give the antitrust agencies the power to authorize unlawful conduct, there are numerous statutory and court made exemptions to United States Antitrust Law. In Armenia, anti-competitive agreements are defined as "contracts and agreements concluded between economic entities or their concerted practices (hereinafter referred to as "agreements"), which might result in the restriction, prevention, prohibition of competition. In Chile, Decree Law No. 211 sets out, in an *illustrative* manner, the acts and contracts that are contrary to free competition (see article 2). Subparagraph (f) of article 2 establishes an "open-ended" concept by stating that: "With regard to the effects provided for in the foregoing article, the following will be considered, inter alia, as facts, acts or agreements tending to impede free competition: (…) Generally, any other measure tending to eliminate, restrict or hinder free competition." Likewise, the jurisprudence of the anti-monopoly bodies considers unfair competition as conduct contrary to competition. In the EC, Agreements restrictive of competition in the sense of Article 81(1) EC are only

automatically void if they are not exempted by Article 81(3) EC. Prohibited are only those agreements which are restrictive of competition in the sense of Article 81(1) and not exempted in the sense of Article 81(3). However, under implementing Regulation No 17, which is currently still in force, the Commission has the exclusive power to decide (upon notification of the agreement to it) that the exemption under Article 81(3) applies. This means that under the current implementation system, a national judge assessing the validity of an agreement, which is restrictive of competition in the sense of Article 81(1), has no other choice than to rule that it is void, unless (a) the Commission has granted an exemption under Article 81(3) or (b) the agreement has at least been notified to the Commission for exemption and the Commission has not decided upon exemption yet (in this latter case the national judge would usually stay his proceedings until the Commission decision). The new implementing Regulation 1/2003, which will enter into force on 1 May 2004, abolishes the Commission's exclusive power to decide upon an exemption under Article 81(3). Instead, this provision will become directly applicable, so that a national judge who assesses an agreement and concludes that it is restrictive of competition in the sense of Article 81(1) will be able and obliged to go further and assess whether the conditions for exemption under Article 81(3) are fulfilled. Depending on his conclusion in this regard he will either rule that the agreement void or is not void under Article 81[83]. In Tunisia, "concerted actions and express or tacit agreements aimed at preventing, restricting or falsifying competition on the market are prohibited when they tend to:

1/ Create an obstacle to the fixing of prices by the free play of supply and demand;

2/ Limit access to the market for other enterprises or the free exercise of competition;

3/ Limit or control production, outlets, investments or technical progress;

4/ Allocate markets or sources of supply."

Other than in exceptional cases authorized by the Minister in charge of trade matters, upon advice from the Competition Council, contracts of concession and exclusive commercial representation are prohibited. Also prohibited is the abuse of a dominant position in the domestic market or a substantial part thereof, or of a state of economic dependence wherein a client enterprise or supplier does not have alternatives for the marketing, supply or provision of a service. Abuse of a dominant position or of a state of economic dependence may consist particularly in refusal to sell or purchase, in tied sales or purchases, in minimum prices imposed with a view to resale, in discriminatory conditions of sale as well as in the termination of commercial relations for no valid reason or for the sole reason that the partner refuses to be subjected to unjustified commercial conditions[84].

In Ukraine, agreements, in any form by economic entities, taking decisions in any form by associations and other concerted competitive behaviour (actions or inactivity) of economic entities, shall be considered as concerted actions. The establishment of an economic entity that is directed towards or results in the co-ordination of competitive behaviour between economic entities or between them and the newly-established economic entity shall also be considered as concerted actions. In Zambia, restrictive agreements or arrangements (referred to in the Act as anti-competitive trade practices) are listed under sections 7, 8, 9 and 10. However, there is an all embracing general description of all such conduct under section 7(1) which states that "any category of agreements, decisions and concerted practices which have as their object the prevention, restriction or distortion of competition to an appreciable extent in Zambia or in any substantial part of it are declared anti-competitive trade practices and are hereby prohibited. Furthermore, the Zambian legislation (section 9) makes it an offence for enterprises engaged on the market in rival or potentially rival activities to engage in arrangements (formal, informal, written and unwritten) that limit access to markets or otherwise unduly restrain competition. However, this does not apply where the enterprises are under common control and consequently do not act independently of each other. In Estonia, permission may be granted if the generally prohibited agreement, concerted practice or decision by associations of undertakings:

1) contributes to improving the production or distribution of goods (or services) or to promoting technical or economic progress or to protecting the environment, while allowing consumers a fair share of the resulting benefit;

2) does not impose on the undertakings which enter into the agreement, engage in concerted practices or adopt the decision any restrictions which are not

indispensable to the attainment of the objectives specified in previous subsection;

3) does not afford the undertakings which enter into the agreement, engage in concerted practices or adopt the decision the possibility of eliminating competition in respect of a substantial part of the relevant market (Estonian Competition Act Article 6). Estonia has enforced same block exemptions as they are in EU.

In the EU, since 2000, a new general block exemption applied to all supply and distribution agreements. This regulation on the one hand exempts up to a market share threshold of 30 % such agreements that can be considered to be efficiency-enhancing. On the other hand, a number of hard core restrictions are excluded from the exemption, in particular in order to ensure the freedom of distributors to set their own prices and in order to ensure that parallel trade can take place and that final consumers can purchase products wherever they want.

Within the EU some of those practices are subject to so-called "block exemption regulations " (not "category exemptions"). Of particular importance is Commission Regulation (EC) No 2790/1999 of 22 December 1999[85]. In South Africa, Section (10)(3)(b) of the South African Competition Act, 1998 provides for public interest grounds upon which an exemption can be granted, but limited to only four. In Tunisia, agreements and practices are not considered as anti-competitive where the authors can show that they have the effect of promoting technical or economic progress and that they provide for the users a fair share of the resulting benefit. These practices are subject to authorization by the Minister in charge of trade matters, upon advice from the Competition Council. In Ukraine, Competition Law contains an exception which specifically relates to small and medium enterprises: "The provisions of Article 6 of the present Law shall not be applied to such voluntary concerted actions of small and medium-sized entrepreneurs in terms of the joint purchase of products that do not result in the substantial restriction of competition and that facilitate raising the competitiveness of the small and medium-sized entrepreneurs." (Art 7). Moreover, Art. 10 states that: "the concerted actions provided for by Article 6 of the Law may be authorised by the relevant bodies of the Antimonopoly Committee of Ukraine if their participants prove that the concerted actions facilitate:

1. The improvement of the production, purchase or sale of a product;

2. Technical, technological, and economic development;

3. The development of small or medium-sized entrepreneurs;

4. The optimisation of the export or import of products;

5. The elaboration and application of unified technical conditions; or

6. Standards for products; the rationalisation of production.

In Zambia, the law recognizes that some objectives of society may not always be met by the operation of competitive markets. The adjudication (Authorisation and Notification) procedures under the Act provide for negative clearance of conduct with demonstrable public benefits that outweigh any anti-competitive detriment.

CHAPTER IV

Acts or behaviour constituting an abuse of a dominant position of market power

I. *Prohibition of acts or behaviour involving an abuse, or acquisition and abuse, of a dominant position of market power*

A prohibition on acts or behaviour involving an abuse or acquisition and abuse of a dominant position of market power:

(i) Where an enterprise, either by itself or acting together with a few other enterprises, is in a position to control a relevant market for a particular good or service, or groups of goods or services;

(ii) Where the acts or behaviour of a dominant enterprise limit access to a relevant market or otherwise unduly restrain competition, having or being likely to have adverse effects on trade or economic development.

II. *Acts or behaviour considered as abusive:*

(a) Predatory behaviour towards competitors, such as using below cost pricing to eliminate competitors;

(b) Discriminatory (i.e. unjustifiably differentiated) pricing or terms or conditions in the supply or purchase of goods or services, including by means of the use of pricing policies in transactions between affiliated enterprises which overcharge or undercharge for goods or services purchased or supplied as compared with prices for similar or comparable transactions outside the affiliated enterprises;

(c) Fixing the prices at which goods sold can be resold, including those imported and exported;

(d) Restrictions on the importation of goods which have been legitimately marked abroad with a trademark identical with or similar to the trademark protected as to identical or similar goods in the importing country where the trademarks in question are of the same origin, i.e. belong to the same owner or are used by enterprises between which there is economic, organizational, managerial or legal interdependence, and where the purpose of such restrictions is to maintain artificially high prices;

(e) When not for ensuring the achievement of legitimate business purposes, such as quality, safety, adequate distribution or service:

(i) Partial or complete refusal to deal on an enterprise's customary commercial terms;

(ii) Making the supply of particular goods or services dependent upon the acceptance of restrictions on the distribution or manufacture of competing or other goods;

(iii) Imposing restrictions concerning where, or to whom, or in what form or quantities, goods supplied or other goods may be resold or exported;

(iv) Making the supply of particular goods or services dependent upon the purchase of other goods or services from the supplier or his designee.

III. *Authorization or exemption*

Acts, practices or transactions not absolutely prohibited by the law may be authorized or exempted if they are notified, as described in article 7, before being put into effect, if all relevant facts are truthfully disclosed to competent authorities, if affected parties have an opportunity to be heard, and if it is then determined that the proposed conduct, as altered or regulated if necessary, will be consistent with the objectives of the law.

COMMENTARIES ON CHAPTER IV AND ALTERNATIVE APPROACHES IN EXISTING LEGISLATIONS

Acts or behaviour constituting an abuse of a dominant position of market power

I.   *Prohibition of acts or behaviour involving an abuse of a dominant position of market power*

A prohibition on acts or behaviour involving an abuse of a dominant position of market power:

(i) Where an enterprise, either by itself or acting together with few other enterprises, is in a position to control a relevant market for a particular good or service, or groups of goods or services;

(ii) Where the acts or behaviour of a dominant enterprise limit access to a relevant market or otherwise unduly restrain competition, having or being likely to have adverse effects on trade or economic development.

53. The elements of this article are based upon section D, paragraph 4, of the Set of Principles and Rules and, as in respect of paragraph I, a prohibition in principle approach has been followed when the conditions described in (i) and (ii) exist. Such a situation will require a case by case analysis to establish whether the acts or behaviour of an enterprise involve an abuse of a dominant position of market power. For a description of the reasoning on the prohibition of abuse of a dominant position of market power, see box 8.

Box 8

Abuse of a dominant position and abuse of market power

The concept of abuse of a dominant position of market power refers to the anti competitive business practices in which a dominant firm may engage in order to maintain or increase its position in the market. The prohibition of abuse of a dominant position and market power has been incorporated in competition legislation in countries such as Canada, Czech Republic, Italy, France, Germany. In EC Competition Law, Article 82 EC applies not only to abuses in which a firm engages in order to maintain or increase its position in the market, i.e. exclusionary abuses, but also to some forms of exploitative abuses such as excessive pricing.

In this concept there are two elements, namely the question of dominance and the ability to exert market power.

· A firm holds a dominant position when it accounts for a significant share of a relevant market and has a significantly larger market share than its next largest rival. When a firm holds market shares of 40 per cent or more, it is usually a dominant firm which can raise competition concerns when it has the capacity to set prices independently and abuse its market power. However, one has to pay attention to the fact that a dominant position in itself is not anti competitive as such.

· Market power represents the ability of a firm (or a group of firms acting jointly) to raise and profitably maintain prices above the level that would prevail under competition for a significant period of time. It is also referred to as monopoly power. The exercise or abuse of a dominant position of market power leads to reduced output and loss of economic welfare. In addition to higher than competitive prices, the exercise of market power can be manifested through reduced quality of service or a lack of innovation in relevant markets.

Factors that tend to create market power include a high degree of market concentration, the existence of barriers to entry and a lack of substitutes for a product supplied by firms whose conduct is under examination by competition authorities. Abuse of a dominant position of market power can vary widely from one sector to another. Abuses include the following: charging unreasonable or excessive prices, price discrimination, predatory pricing, refusal to deal or to sell, tied selling or product bundling, pre emption of facilities, etc.

54. The concept of dominance and its use in practice may not necessarily be the same for merger cases and abuse cases. Indeed, merger control is based on a prospective analysis whilst abuse cases are assessed on the basis of past practice of an undertaking[86]. A dominant position of market power refers to the degree of actual or potential control of the market by an enterprise or enterprises acting together, or forming an economic entity, or, in other words, acting independently of other operators in that market. The control can be measured on the basis of market shares, total annual turnover, size of assets, number of employees, etc.; also it should focus on the ability of a firm or firms to raise prices above (or depress prices below) the competitive level for a significant period of time. In certain countries, the law specifies the market share which the enterprise or enterprises must hold in order to be considered in a dominant position or a monopolistic situation, and, depending on the country, it is used either as a jurisdictional hurdle for initiating investigations or as critical market share where firms are obliged to notify the Authority. The Indian Competition Act 2002 defines, 'dominant position' as a position of strength, enjoyed by an enterprise, in the relevant market, in India, which enables it to: (i) operate independently of competitive forces prevailing in the relevant market; or (ii) affect its competitors or consumers or the relevant market in its favour. The Competition Commission of India, while inquiring whether an enterprise enjoys a dominant position or not, has due regard to all or any of these factors. In Poland, the law presumes a firm might have "a dominant position, when its market share exceeds 40 per cent"[87]. The presumption contained in the 1991 Law of the Czech Republic is of 40%, which is also the case of Portugal. In the Czech Republic, provided that the other indicators, mentioned in the Act, do not show otherwise, a competitor or competitors with joint dominance that have not achieved the market share of 40% in a given period are considered not to have a dominant position on a market[88]. The legislations of Mongolia, and Ukraine consider that dominance exists when a single entity acting alone or a group of economic entities acting together account constantly for over 50 per cent of supply to the market of a certain good or similar goods, products or carried out works and provided services[89].

Under Canadian law, joint dominance can be proven indirectly. The word "together" in chapter IV (i) suggests an idea of complicity of a criminal nature, hence involving a greater burden of proof. According to Canadian law, this article goes beyond the current requirements in terms of its scope of application.

In Canada, section 4 does not incorporate the requirements as to effects. The wording "unduly restrain competition" is used for infringements of a criminal nature and "adverse effect" for refusal to sell. As to the abuse of dominant position, the test here is more demanding: it must rather be shown that the practice has had, is having or is likely to have the effect of preventing or lessening competition substantially for tied selling.

Section 4 includes under the abuse of dominance some restrictive trade practices such as the refusal to deal, exclusive dealing and market restrictions and tied selling. Although these practices could be reviewed under the abuse of dominance provisions of the Canadian Competition Act (section 79), these restrictive practices were incorporated under specific civil provisions which require different substantive tests to be met and could be addressed under these provisions where they might not meet the competition test under Canadian Competition Act (Section 79). In this connection, the proof of abuse of dominance requires that the business conduct has had, is having or is likely to have the effect of preventing or lessening competition substantially, while under refusal to deal, the proof that a person is substantially affected or precluded from carrying on business due to his inability to obtain adequate supplies of a product, is willing to meet the usual trade terms of the supplier, the product is in ample supply and the refusal is having or is likely to have an adverse effect on competition has to be established.

55. Furthermore, Section 79 of the Canadian Competition Act addresses the situation where a firm might not control a market and consequently might be disregarded under the abuse of dominance but nevertheless adopt a restrictive practice that needs to be addressed. Also, under practices of tied selling and exclusive dealing, one has to establish that the practice has been engaged in by a major supplier or be widespread in a market and that the practice is likely to impede entry or expansion of a firm, or sales of a product, in the market or have some other exclusionary effect, with the effect that competition is or is likely to be lessened substantially[90].

56. Under the Lithuanian law, a 40 per cent market share establishes a presumption of dominance, in addition, the new law creates a presumption of joint dominance when the three largest firms in a market have a collective market share of 70 per cent. In the case of the

Russian Federation[91], the law refers to 65 per cent. "In Germany, the legislation contains several presumptions, namely: at least one enterprise has one third of a certain type of goods or commercial services, and a turnover of at least DM 250 million in the last completed business year; three or fewer enterprises have a combined market share of 50 per cent or over; five or fewer enterprises have a combined market share of two thirds or over. This presumption does not apply to enterprises which record turnovers less than DM 100 million in the last completed business year"[92]. In the "Akzo" *Judgement*, the Court of Justice of the European Communities considered that highly important parts (of the market) are by themselves, except for extraordinary circumstances, the sole proof of the existence of a dominant position[93]. In Estonia, an undertaking in a dominant position is an undertaking which accounts for at least 40 per cent of the turnover in the relevant market or whose position enables the undertaking to operate in the market to an appreciable extent independently of competitors, suppliers and buyers. Undertakings with special or exclusive rights or in control of essential facilities are also undertakings in a dominant position.

57. In Zambia, under section 7 (2) of the Act, abuse of dominant power is expressed as acts or behaviour that limit access to markets or otherwise unduly restrain competition, or have or are likely to have adverse effects on trade or the economy in general. Generally, an enterprise is considered to be dominant if it has a level of market power that allows it to behave independently of competitive pressures (e.g. pricing and distribution strategies). An important but not conclusive factor in determining dominance is the share of the market that the undertaking has. An undertaking is unlikely to be dominant if its market share is less than 40% - although this rule will largely depend on the circumstances of the case. The abuse of a dominant position is one key element of the Act. For the provision to apply, one or more persons must substantially control a class of business throughout Zambia or a substantial part of it, and have engaged in or currently be engaging in a practice of anti-competitive conduct that has the effect of preventing or lessening competition substantially.

58. In the Zambian legislation, acts or behaviour considered as abusive are listed under section 7(2) of the Act and are said to have the likely effect to limit access to markets (barriers to entry) or otherwise unduly restrain competition, or have or are likely to have adverse effects on trade or the economy in general. The acts

include predatory pricing, discriminatory pricing, exclusive dealing, tied selling, full line forcing and territorial restraint, anticompetitive acquisitions of any sort, and collusion in pricing in order to eliminate competition. All these are prohibited in principle but can be authorized under the authorization and notification process.

59. The Zambian legislation provides for authorisation and notification of acts that, though anti-competitive, have reasonable public benefits that outweigh any anti-competitive detriment. This excludes matters that affect consumers. It is solely up to the applicants to prove the benefits anticipated. Key industry interested parties and other stakeholders are consulted before the Commission reaches its decision[94].

60. Specific criteria defining market dominance, however, can be difficult to lay down. In the United States, for instance, monopoly power is not defined by statute but courts have traditionally defined it as being "the power to control market prices or exclude competition." United States v. E.I. du Pont de Nemours & Co., 351 U.S. 377, 391 (1956). Market share is not the only factor considered in determining whether monopoly power exists. Other factors, such as the absence of entry barriers, may indicate that a firm does not have monopoly power even if it does account for a large share of the relevant market. In the Michelin *Judgement*, the Court of Justice of the European Communities stated that under article *82* of the EEC Treaty a dominant position refers to a situation of economic strength, which gives the enterprise the power to obstruct the maintenance of an effective competition in the market concerned and because it allows the enterprise to conduct itself in a way that is independent from its competitors, clients and, finally, consumers[95]. In addition to market share, the structural advantages possessed by enterprises can be of decisive importance. For example, the Court of Justice of the European Communities in the United Brands Judgement took into account the fact that the undertaking possessed a high degree of vertical integration, that its advertising policy hinged on a specific brand ("Chiquita"), guaranteeing it a steady supply of customers and that it controlled every stage of the distribution process, which together gave the corporation a considerable advantage over its competitors[96]. In consequence, dominance can derive from a combination of a number of factors which, if taken separately, would not necessarily be determinative.

61. A dominant position of market power refers not only to the position of one enterprise but also to the situation where two or more enterprises acting together could wield control. This clearly refers to highly concentrated markets such as in an oligopoly, where Two or more enterprises control a large share of the market, thus creating and enjoying conditions through which they can dominate or operate on the market very much in the same manner as would a monopolist. The same criterion was adopted by the European Commission and the Court of First Instance of the European Communities in the Vetro Piano in Italia Judgement[97], which was soon

---

Box 9

Barriers to entry in competition law and policy

Barriers to entry to a market refer to a number of factors which may prevent or deter the entry of new firms into an industry even when incumbent firms are earning excess profits. There are two broad classes of barriers: structural (or economic) and strategic (or behavioural).

· *Structural barriers to entry* arise from basic industry characteristics such as technology, cost and demand. There is some debate over what factors constitute relevant structural barriers. The widest definition suggests that barriers to entry arise from product differentiation, absolute cost advantages of incumbents, and economies of scale. Product differentiation creates advantages for incumbents because entrants must overcome the accumulated brand loyalty of existing products. Absolute cost advantages imply that the entrant will enter with higher unit costs at every rate of output, perhaps because of inferior technology. Scale economies restrict the number of firms which can operate at minimum costs in a market of given size. A narrower definition of structural barriers to entry has been given by George Stigler and the proponents of the Chicago school of antitrust analysis. They suggest that barriers to entry arise only when an entrant must incur costs which incumbents do not bear. Therefore, this definition excludes scale economies and advertising expenses as barriers (because these are costs which incumbents have had to sustain in order to attain their position in the market). Other economists also emphasize the importance of sunk costs as a barrier to entry. Since such costs must be incurred by entrants, but have already been borne by incumbents, a barrier to entry is created. In addition, sunk costs reduce the ability to exit and thus impose extra risks on potential entrants.

· *Strategic barriers to entry* refer to the behaviour of incumbents. In particular, incumbents may act so as to heighten structural barriers to entry or threaten to retaliate against entrants if they do enter. Such threats must, however, be credible in the sense that incumbents must have an incentive to carry them out if entry does not occur. Strategic entry deterrence often involves some kind of pre emptive behaviour by incumbents. One example is the pre emption of facilities by which an incumbent over invests in capacity in order to threaten a price war if entry actually occurs. Another would be the artificial creation of new brands and products in order to limit the possibility of imitation. This possibility remains subject to debate. Lastly, Governments can also be a source of barriers to entry in an industry through licensing and other regulations.

Barriers to entry into a specific industry can vary widely according to the level of maturity or of development of a market. Estimated barriers to entry for some selected industries in a mature economy include the following:

High barriers to entry	**Moderately high barriers to entry**	**Low barriers to entry**
Electric generation and distribution	Bakery	Meat packing
Local telephone service	Soft drinks	Flour
Newspapers	Cigarettes	Canned fruits and vegetables
Branded soaps	Periodicals	Woollen and cotton textiles
Aircraft and parts	Gypsum products	Clothing
Automobile industry	Organic chemicals	Small metal products
Mainframe computers	Toilet preparations	Wooden furniture
Heavy electrical equipment	Petroleum refining	Corrugated containers
Locomotives	Aluminium	Printing
Beer	Heavy industrial machinery	Footwear
Cereals	Large household appliances	Trucking and road transportation
	Railroad transportation	

Sources: UNCTAD; and W. Shepherd, *The Economics of Industrial Organization*. Englewood Cliffs, 1990.

followed by the Nestlé Perrier merger case[98]. In consequence, the cumulative effect of use of a particular practice, such as tying agreements, may well result in an abuse of a dominant position. In the United Kingdom, "complex monopoly" provisions are not necessarily limited to oligopoly situations[99].

62. The abuse or acquisition and abuse of a dominant position are two closely interrelated concepts, namely the abuse of a dominant position of market power, and the acquisition and abuse of such power. See commentary to Article 5.

63. Subsections (a) to (f) section II, Article 3 indicate the behaviour considered *prima facie* abusive when an enterprise is in a dominant position. As such, the inquiry concerns an examination of the conduct of the market dominating enterprise(s) rather than a challenge of its dominance. However, the maintenance and exercise of such power through abusive behaviour is challenged.

64. It should be noted that in the United States, case law has shifted generally towards more favourable evaluation of vertical restraints primarily because they offer the potential for stimulating interbrand competition[100]. For the treatment of vertical restraints by competition law, see box 5 above.

II.   *Acts or behaviour considered as abusive*

65. Usually, competition laws provide only some examples of behaviours which are considered abusive and prohibited. These behaviours include a whole range of firm strategies aimed at raising barriers to entry to a market. Such barriers to entry are factors which prevent or deter the entry of new firms into an industry even when incumbent firms are earning excess profits. For a description of barriers to entry see box 9.

(a) Predatory behaviour towards competitors, such as using below cost pricing to eliminate competitors;

66. One of the most common forms of predatory behaviour is generally referred to as predatory pricing. Enterprises engage in such behaviour to drive competing enterprises out of business, with the intention of maintaining or strengthening a dominant position. The greater the diversification of the activities of the enterprise in terms of products and markets and the greater its financial resources, the greater is its ability to

engage in predatory behaviour. An example of regulations on predatory pricing appears in the People's Republic of China Law for Countering Unfair Competition. It states that an operator (i.e. enterprises or individuals) may not sell its or his goods at a price that is below the cost for the purpose of excluding its or his competitors[101]. Also, the legislation of Mongolia forbids an enterprise to sell its own goods at a price lower than the cost, with the intention of impeding the entry of other economic entities into the market or driving them from the market[102]. Hungary follows a similar criterion; it prohibits the setting of extremely low prices which are not based on greater efficiency in comparison with that of competitors and are likely to drive out competitors from the relevant market or to hinder their market entry[103]. In the United States, the Supreme Court has held that two elements must be present in order to establish predatory pricing. First, the prices complained of must be "below an appropriate measure of cost," and second, the competitor charging low prices must have a "dangerous probability" of recouping its investment in below-cost prices. Brooke Group Ltd. v. Brown & Williamson Tobacco Corp., 509 U.S. (1993). See also Cargill Inc. v. Monfort of Colo., Inc., 479 U.S. 104, 117 (1986). The US Supreme Court has stated that it is important to distinguish between pro-competitive price-cutting and anti-competitive predatory pricing because "cutting prices in order to increase business often is the very essence of competition." Matsushita Elec. Indus. Co. v. Zenith Radio Corp., 475 U.S. 574, 594 (1986).

67. Predatory behaviour is not limited to pricing. Other means, such as acquisition with a view to the suspension of activities of a competitor, can be considered as predatory behaviour[104]. So can excessive pricing, or the refusal of an enterprise in a dominant position to supply a material essential for the production activities of a customer who is in a position to engage in competitive activities. For a description of various types of price discrimination, see box 10.

(b) Discriminatory (i.e. unjustifiably differentiated) pricing or terms or conditions in the supply or purchase of goods or services, including by means of the use of pricing policies in transactions between affiliated enterprises which overcharge or undercharge for goods or services purchased or supplied as compared with prices for similar or comparable transactions outside the affiliated enterprises;

68. Closely related to predatory pricing is the practice of discriminatory pricing. While below cost pricing vis à vis

Box 10

Types of price discrimination

Price discrimination is an indispensable tool for firms to maximize their profits from whatever market position they hold and raise or defend that position against other firms. However discrimination can also be used by holders of market power to avoid competition by increasing market shares and/or barriers to entry. Price discrimination cases must be carefully examined by competition authorities. There are several types of price discrimination, some of which do stimulate the competitive process. They may be listed in three categories, some practices having a strong relation to international trade and economic relations and some being evidence of economic efficiency:

(a)   Personal discrimination

·   *Haggle every time*: Dealing common in bazaars and private deals.

·   *Size up his income*: Pricing related to the customer's purchasing power, frequent for doctors, lawyers and members of the "professions".

·   *Measure the use*: Even if marginal costs are low, charge heavy customers more (large dominant computer, software and copier manufacturers are known to have used this strategy).

(b)   Group discrimination

·   *Kill the rival*: Predatory price cutting aimed at driving out a competitor. Said to have been commonly used by American Tobacco and Standard Oil.

·   *Dump the surplus*: Selling at lower prices in foreign markets where demand is more elastic. Common for some drugs, steel, TV sets and other goods, but complaints about dumping are often unsuccessful.

·   *Promote new customers*: Common with magazine subscriptions, luring new customers. Often promotes competition where operators do not dominate the market.

·   *Favour the big ones*: Volume discounts are steeper than cost differences. Very frequent in many markets, especially in utilities.

·   *Divide them by elasticity*: Common in utilities.

(c) Product discrimination

·   *Pay for the label*: The premium label (or most notorious) gets a higher price, even if the good is the same as a common brand.

·   *Clear the stock*: "Sales" which are commonly used to clear the inventory but which may also destabilize consumers and competitors if resulting from false advertising.

·   *Peak off peak differences*: Prices may differ by more or less than costs do, between peak hour congested times and slack off periods. Nearly universal in utilities.

To assess the pro or anti competitive nature of discrimination, the competition authority will evaluate the legality of the practice with reference to its economic effects on the relevant markets and to the position of the operators in those markets. In many jurisdictions, vertical restraints are subject to a "rule of reason" approach, reflecting the fact that such restraints are not always harmful and may in fact be beneficial in particular market structures or circumstances.

Sources: F. Machlup, *The Political Economy of Monopoly*. Baltimore, 1952; W. Shepherd, *The Economics of Industrial Organization*. Englewood Cliffs, 1990.

direct competitors may be predatory, discriminatory pricing can also be predatory, as for example in the case of discounts based on quantities, "bonus systems" or "fidelity discounts"[105]. In this situation, irrespective of injury to direct competitors, discriminatory pricing can injure competitors of the favoured purchaser[106]. In spite of what has been mentioned, it is also important to point out that in many cases quantity discounts often reflect reduced transaction costs or have the purpose of meeting competition, and should not be discouraged. Injury to competitors of the favoured purchaser should not in and of itself concern competition authorities, because competition laws should protect competition and not competitors.

69. In Peru, although the legislation considers discriminatory pricing as an example of abusive behaviour, discounts and bonuses that correspond to generally accepted commercial practices that are given because of special circumstances such as anticipated payment, quantity, volume, etc., and when they are granted in similar conditions to all consumers, do not constitute a case of abuse of dominant position[107].

70. Other types of price based discrimination would include "delivered pricing", i.e. selling at uniform price irrespective of location (whatever the transportation costs to the seller), and "base point selling", where one area has been designated as base point (whereby the seller charges transportation fees from that point irrespective of the actual point of shipment and its costs).

71. The proscription of discrimination also includes terms and conditions in the supply or purchase of goods or services. For example, the extension of differentiated credit facilities or ancillary services in the supply of goods and services can also be discriminatory. In the Australian legislation, the prohibition of discrimination is not limited to price based discriminations, but refers also to credits, provision of services and payment for services provided in respect of the goods[108]. It is also to point out that differential terms and conditions should not be considered unlawful if they are related to cost differences. More generally, preventing firms from offering lower prices to some customers may well result in discouraging firms from cutting prices to anyone. However, the Australian Trade Practices Act 1974 was repealed in 1995 and conduct that would have been considered prohibited under Section 49 can instead be addressed by s.45 if it results in a substantial lessening of competition, or under s.46 if it is a result of the misuse of market power by a corporation. In the Russian Federation, Article (5) of the Law prohibits conduct and agreements by firms that restrict competition.

72. Undercharging for goods or services in transactions between affiliated enterprises (a case of transfer pricing) can be used as a means of predation against competitors who are not able to obtain supplies at comparable prices.

(c) Fixing the prices at which goods sold can be resold, including those imported and exported;

73. Fixing the resale price of goods, usually by the manufacturer or by the wholesaler, is generally termed resale price maintenance (RPM). Resale price maintenance is prohibited in many countries, such as for example India, New Zealand, Republic of Korea, the United Kingdom. In the United States, the Supreme Court has held that minimum resale price maintenance is per se illegal under Section One of the Sherman Act, but there must be an actual agreement requiring the distributor to adhere to specific prices. See Business Elecs. Corp. v. Sharp Elecs. Corp., 485 U.S. 717, 720, 724 (1988). Because maximum resale price maintenance may lead to low prices, the Supreme Court has recently ruled that maximum resale price maintenance is not per se an offence. In Sweden an economic approach has been chosen concerning resale price maintenance. Setting minimum prices with an appreciable effect on competition is caught by the prohibition against anti-competitive co-operation as laid down in the Swedish Competition Act. However, setting maximum prices is not generally prohibited[109]. In the European Community, fixing the resale price of goods is normally prohibited if competition between member States is affected.

74. While the imposition of a resale price is proscribed, legislation in some States does not ban maximum resale prices nor recommended prices (i.e. the United Kingdom and the United States). In the United Kingdom, although recommended resale prices are not proscribed, the Director General of Fair Trading may prohibit the misleading use of recommended prices, for example where unduly high prices are recommended in order to draw attention to apparently large price cuts[110]. In Canada, the publication by a product supplier of an advertisement that mentions a resale price for the product is considered to be an attempt to influence the selling price upwards, unless it is made clear that the product may be sold at a lower price[111].

75. It should be noted that collective resale price maintenance would, when involving competing enterprises (i.e. wholesalers) be covered by article 3, I (a) proposed above as a type of price fixing arrangement.

76. Refusals to deal are generally the most commonly used form of pressure for compliance. For avoiding this situation, for example, the Commission of the European

Communities fined a United States corporation and three of its subsidiaries in Europe for having placed an export ban, in respect of its product (pregnancy tests), on their dealers in one of the European countries (United Kingdom) where such products were sold at considerably lower prices than in another European country (Federal Republic of Germany) concerned[112]. Canadian legislation expressly prohibits refusing to supply a product to a person or class of persons because of their low pricing policy.

(d) Restrictions on the importation of goods which have been legitimately marked abroad with a trademark identical with or similar to the trademark protected as to identical or similar goods in the importing country where the trademarks in question are of the same origin, i.e. belong to the same owner or are used by enterprises between which there is economic, organizational, managerial or legal interdependence, and where the purpose of such restrictions is to maintain artificially high prices;

77. This practice by a dominant firm is prohibited in the Set in section D.4 (e). The owner of a trademark may obtain market power through heavy advertising and other marketing practices. If the trademark in question acquires wide acceptance and wide distribution, the trademark owner can be in a position to impose a wide range of RBPs on the distributors of products bearing its trademark. Trademarks can be used to enforce exclusive dealing arrangements, to exclude imports, allocate markets and, at times, to charge excessive prices. Nevertheless, it should be noted that there are various valid reasons why enterprises might limit distribution of their market products, such as maintaining quality and preventing counterfeiting. These measures are designed to protect legitimate intellectual property rights as well as consumers.

78. With regard to restricting the importation of goods, the owner of a trademark may seek to prevent imports of the trademarked product; to prevent anybody other than his exclusive distributor from importing the goods (parallel imports), to prevent similar products bearing his trademark from being imported in competition with his own products, and to use different trademarks for the same product in different countries, thereby preventing imports from one another.

79. In Japan, for example, Old Parr Co. instructed its agents not to supply its whisky to dealers who imported Old Parr whisky from other sources, or who sold the imported products at less than the company's standard price. It devised a special checking mark for packaging supplied by its agents in order to detect any dealer not complying with its requirements. The Japanese Fair Trade Commission investigated the case and found that such action constituted an unfair business practice and accordingly ordered Old Parr to discontinue its practice[113].

80. Concerning restrictions on the importation of similar products legitimately bearing an identical or similar trademark, an example is the Cinzano case in the Federal Republic of Germany. In this case the Federal Supreme Court decided that when a trademark owner has authorized its subsidiaries or independent licensees in different countries to use his mark and sell the goods to which the mark is affixed, the owner may not in such circumstances prohibit importation of products when placed on the market abroad by its foreign subsidiaries or licensees and irrespective of whether the goods differ in quality from the goods of the domestic trademark owner[114].

81. As indicated above, a trademark registered in two or more countries can originate from the same source. In the case of trademarked products exported to other countries but not manufactured there, the trademark is frequently licensed to the exclusive distributor. For example, Watts Ltd. of the United Kingdom, a producer of record maintenance goods, and its exclusive distributor and trademark licensee in the Netherlands, the Theal B.V. (later renamed Tepea B.V.), were fined by the Commission of the European Communities for using its trademark to prevent parallel imports into the Netherlands. The Commission found that the exclusive distribution agreements were designed to ensure absolute territorial protection for Theal by excluding all parallel imports of authentic products, and this protection was strengthened by the prohibition on exports imposed by Watts on wholesalers in the United Kingdom. The system, taken as a whole, left Theal completely free in the Netherlands to fix prices for imported products[115].

82. The fourth type of case concerns the use of two different trademarks for the same product in different countries in order to achieve market fragmentation. In an action brought by Centrafarm B.V. against American Home Products Corporation (AHP), Centrafarm claimed that, as a parallel importer, it was entitled to sell without authorization in the Netherlands, under the trade name "Seresta", oxazepamum tablets originating from AHP Corporation and offered for sale in the United Kingdom

under the name "Serenid D", since the drugs were identical. In this case, the Court ruled that the exercise of such a right can constitute a disguised restriction on trade in the EEC if it is established that a practice of using different marks for the same product, or preventing the use of a trademark name on repackaged goods, was adopted in order to achieve partition of markets and to maintain artificially high prices[116].

(e) When not for ensuring the achievement of legitimate business purposes, such as quality, safety, adequate distribution or service:

  (i) Partial or complete refusal to deal on an enterprise's customary commercial terms;

  (ii) Making the supply of particular goods or services dependent upon the acceptance of restrictions on the distribution or manufacture of competing or other goods;

  (iii) Imposing restrictions concerning where, or to whom, or in what form or quantities, goods supplied or other goods may be resold or exported;

  (iv) Making the supply of particular goods or services dependent upon the purchase of other goods or services from the supplier or his designee.

83. While prohibited in principle, possible authorization has been envisaged for behaviour listed in sub articles (i) to (iv) when it is for ensuring the achievement of legitimate business purposes such as safety, quality, adequate distribution or service provided it is not inconsistent with the objective of the law. Governments set standards in order to ensure adequate health, safety and quality. However, when enterprises claim such standards as justification for engaging in exclusionary practices, particularly when in a dominant position, it gives rise to suspicion as to the purpose of such practices, i.e. whether or not the intent is monopolistic. It is even more suspect when enterprises set standards of their own volition and claim quality considerations as justification for the use of such practices as refusals to deal, tied selling and selective distribution arrangements. Agreements on standards among competitors, if they restricted access to markets, would be subject to article 3. In the "Tetra Pak" and "Hilti" cases, the European Commission considered that an enterprise having a dominant position is not entitled to substitute public authorities in carrying out a tied in sales policy base or claiming security of health reasons. In both cases the

Commission's position was confirmed[117].

84. As a general rule, the inquiry regarding exclusionary behaviour should entail an examination of the position of the relevant enterprises in the market, the structure of the market, and the probable effects of such exclusionary practices on competition as well as on trade or economic development.

  (i) Partial or complete refusal to deal on an enterprise's customary commercial terms;

85. A refusal to deal may seem like an inherent right, since theoretically only the seller or the buyer is affected by his refusal to sell or buy. However, in reality the motives for refusing to sell can be manifold and are often used by dominant firms to enforce other practices such as resale price maintenance or selective distribution arrangements. In addition, refusals to sell can be intimately related to an enterprise's dominant position in the market and are often used as a means of exerting pressure on enterprises to maintain resale prices.

86. Refusals to deal that are intended to enforce potentially anti competitive restraints, such as resale price maintenance and selective distribution arrangements, raise obvious competitive concerns. Refusals to deal, however, are not in and of themselves anti competitive, and firms should be free to choose to deal, and also give preferential treatment, to traditional buyers, related enterprises, dealers that make timely payments for the goods they buy, or who will maintain the quality, image, etc. of the manufacturer's product. Also it is the case when the enterprise announces in advance the circumstances under which he will refuse to sell (i.e. merely indicating his wishes concerning a retail price and declining further dealings with all who fail to observe them). In this context the United States Supreme Court had ruled that "the purpose of the Sherman Act is to prohibit monopolies, contracts and combinations which probably would unduly interfere with the free exercise of their rights by those engaged, or who wish to engage, in trade and commerce in a word to preserve the right of freedom to trade. In the absence of any purpose to create or maintain a monopoly, the act does not restrict the long recognized right of a trader or manufacturer engaged in an entirely private business freely to exercise his own independent discretion as to parties with whom he will deal; and of course, he may announce in advance the circumstances under which he will refuse to sell"[118].

(ii) Making the supply of particular goods or services dependent upon the acceptance of restrictions on the distribution or manufacture of competing or other goods;

87. Such behaviour is frequently an aspect of "exclusive dealing arrangements", and can be described as a commercial practice whereby an enterprise receives the exclusive rights, frequently within a designated territory, to buy, sell or resell another enterprise's goods or services. As a condition for such exclusive rights, the seller frequently requires the buyer not to deal in, or manufacture, competing goods.

88. Under such arrangements, the distributor relinquishes part of his commercial freedom in exchange for protection from sales of the specific product in question by competitors. The terms of the agreement normally reflect the relative bargaining position of the parties involved.

89. The results of such restrictions are similar to that achieved through vertical integration within an economic entity, the distributive outlet being controlled by the supplier but, in the former instance, without bringing the distributor under common ownership.

(iii) Imposing restrictions concerning where, or to whom, or in what form or quantities, goods supplied or other goods may be resold or exported;

90. Arrangements between the supplier and his distributor often involve the allocation of a specific territory (territorial allocations) or specific type of customer (customer allocations), i.e. where and with whom the distributor can deal. For example, the distributor might be restricted to sales of the product in question in bulk from the wholesalers or only to selling directly to retail outlets. The purpose of such restrictions is usually to minimize intra brand competition by blocking parallel trade by third parties. The effects of such restrictions are manifested in prices and conditions of sale, particularly in the absence of strong inter brand competition in the market. Nevertheless, restrictions on intra brand competition may be benign or pro competitive if the market concerned has significant competition between brands[119]. In the United States, where agreements have been challenged as unlawful exclusive dealing, the courts have typically condemned only those arrangements that substantially foreclose competition in a relevant market by significantly reducing the number of outlets available

to a competitor to reach prospective consumers of the competitor's product. See Tampa Electric Co. v. Nashville Coal Co., 365 U.S. 320, 327 (1961); Roland Machinery Co. v. Dresser Industries, Inc., 749 F.2d 380, 393 (7th Cir. 1984).

91. Territorial allocations can take the form of designating a certain territory to the distributor by the supplier, the understanding being that the distributor will not sell to customers outside that territory, nor to customers which may, in turn, sell the products in another area of the country.

92. Customer allocations are related to the case in which the supplier requires the buyer to sell only to a particular class of customers, for example, only to retailers. Reasons for such a requirement are the desire of the manufacturer to maintain or promote product image or quality, or that the supplier may wish to retain for himself bulk sales to large purchasers, such as sales of vehicles to fleet users or sales to the government. Customer allocations may also be designed to restrict final sales to certain outlets, for example approved retailers meeting certain conditions. Such restrictions can be designed to withhold supplies from discount retailers or independent retailers for the purpose of maintaining resale prices and limiting sales and service outlets.

93. Territorial and customer allocation arrangements serve to enforce exclusive dealing arrangements which enable suppliers, when in a dominant position in respect of the supply of the product in question, to insulate particular markets one from another and thereby engage in differential pricing according to the level that each market can bear. Moreover, selective distribution systems are frequently designed to prevent resale through export outside the designated territory for fear of price competition in areas where prices are set at the highest level.

(iv) Making the supply of particular goods or services dependent upon the purchase of other goods or services from the supplier or his designee.

94. Such behaviour is generally referred to as tied selling. The "tied" product may be totally unrelated to the product requested or a product in a similar line[120]. Tying arrangements are normally imposed in order to promote the sale of slower moving products and in particular those subject to greater competition from substitute products. By virtue of the dominant position of the supplier in

respect of the requested product, he is able to impose as a condition for its sale the acceptance of the other products. This can be achieved, for example, through providing fidelity rebates based upon aggregate purchases of the supplying enterprise's complete range of products[121].

95. It should be noted that conditioning the ability of a licensee to license one or more items of intellectual property on the licensee's purchase of another item of intellectual property or a good or a service has been held in some cases to constitute illegal tying in the United States. As noted in Section 5.3 of the Antitrust Guidelines for the Licensing of Intellectual Property, issued by the U.S. Department of Justice and the Federal Trade Commission on 6 April, 1995, the US antitrust agencies would be likely to challenge a tying arrangement if: (1) the seller has market power in the tying product, (2) the arrangement has an adverse effect on competition in the relevant market for the tied product, and (3) efficiency justifications for the arrangement do not outweigh the anticompetitive effects. The Agencies will not presume that a patent, copyright, or trade secret necessarily confers market power upon its owner. This practice is prohibited in almost all legislation worldwide, including in Algeria[122], Hungary[123], Mongolia[124], Switzerland[125] and the MERCOSUR[126].

III.   *Authorization or exemption*

Acts, practices or transactions not absolutely prohibited by the law may be authorized if they are notified, as described in possible elements for article 6, before being put into effect, if all relevant facts are truthfully disclosed to competent authorities, if affected parties have an opportunity to be heard, and if it is then determined that the proposed conduct, as altered or regulated if necessary, will be consistent with the objectives of the law.

96. The Set of Principles and Rules lays down that whether acts or behaviour are abusive should be examined in terms of their purpose and effects in the actual situation. In doing this, it is clearly the responsibility of enterprises to advance evidence to prove the appropriateness of their behaviour in a given circumstance and the responsibility of the national authorities to accept it or not. Generally, in respect of the practices listed under (a) to (d) it is unlikely that, when a firm is in a dominant position, their use would be regarded as appropriate given their likely effects on competition and trade or on economic development.

97. In the Czech Republic one or more undertakings jointly (joint dominance) are deemed to have a dominant position on relevant market, if their market power enables them to behave to significant extent independently of other undertakings or consumers. Market power is assessed according to the amount formulation of ascertained volume of supplies or purchases on the relevant market for the goods in question (market share), achieved by the relevant undertaking or undertakings in joint dominant position during the period examined pursuant to the Law, and pursuant to other indices, in particular the economic and financial power of the undertakings, legal or other barriers to entry into market by other undertakings, vertical integration level of the undertakings, market structure and size of the market shares of their immediate competitors. Furthermore, the law provide for a refutable assumption that an undertaking or undertakings in joint dominance shall be deemed not to be in dominant position, if its/their share on the relevant market achieved during examined period is below 40%[127].

CHAPTER V

Notification

I.   *Notification by enterprises*

1. When practices fall within the scope of articles 3 and 4 and are not prohibited outright, and hence the possibility exists for their authorization, enterprises could be required to notify the practices to the Administering Authority, providing full details as requested.

2. Notification could be made to the Administering Authority by all the parties concerned, or by one or more of the parties acting on behalf of the others, or by any persons properly authorized to act on their behalf.

3. It could be possible for a single agreement to be notified where an enterprise or person is party to restrictive agreements on the same terms with a number of different parties, provided that particulars are also given of all parties, or intended parties, to such agreements.

4. Notification could be made to the Administering Authority where any agreement, arrangement or situation notified under the provisions of the law has been subject to change either in respect of its terms or in respect of the parties, or has been terminated (otherwise than by

affluxion of time), or has been abandoned, or if there has been a substantial change in the situation (within (...) days/months of the event) (immediately).

5. Enterprises could be allowed to seek authorization for agreements or arrangements falling within the scope of articles 3 and 4, and existing on the date of the coming into force of the law, with the provison that they be notified within (...) days/months) of such date.

6. The coming into force of agreements notified could depend upon the granting of authorization, or upon expiry of the time period set for such authorization, or provisionally upon notification.

7. All agreements or arrangements not notified could be made subject to the full sanctions of the law, rather than mere revision, if later discovered and deemed illegal.

II. Action by the Administering Authority

1. Decision by the Administering Authority (within (...) days/months of the receipt of full notification of all details), whether authorization is to be denied, granted or granted subject where appropriate to the fulfillment of conditions and obligations.

2. Periodical review procedure for authorizations granted every (...) months/years, with the possibility of extension, suspension, or the subjecting of an extension to the fulfillment of conditions and obligations.

3. The possibility of withdrawing an authorization could be provided, for instance, if it comes to the attention of the Administering Authority that:

(a) The circumstances justifying the granting of the authorization have ceased to exist;

(b) The enterprises have failed to meet the conditions and obligations stipulated for the granting of the authorization;

(c) Information provided in seeking the authorization was false or misleading.

COMMENTARIES ON CHAPTER V AND ALTERNATIVE APPROACHES IN EXISTING LEGISLATIONS

Notification

I. *Notification by enterprises*

1. When practices fall within the scope of articles 3 and 4 and are not prohibited outright, and hence the possibility exists for their authorization, enterprises could be required to notify the practices to the Administering Authority, providing full details as requested.

2. Notification could be made to the Administering Authority by all the parties concerned, or by one or more of the parties acting on behalf of the others, or by any persons properly authorized to act on their behalf.

3. It could be possible for a single agreement to be notified where an enterprise or person is party to restrictive agreements on the same terms with a number of different parties, provided that particulars are also given of all parties, or intended parties, to such agreements.

4. Notification could be made to the Administering Authority where any agreement, arrangement or situation notified under the provisions of the law has been subject to change either in respect of its terms or in respect of the parties, or has been terminated (otherwise than by affluxion of time), or has been abandoned, or if there has been a substantial change in the situation (within (...) days/months of the event) (immediately).

5. Enterprises could be allowed to seek authorization for agreements or arrangements falling within the scope of articles 3 and 4, and existing on the date of the coming into force of the law, with the provison that they be notified within (...) days/ months) of such date.

6. The coming into force of agreements notified could depend upon the granting of authorization, or upon expiry of the time period set for such authorization, or provisionally upon notification.

7. All agreements or arrangements not notified could be made subject to the full sanctions of the law, rather than mere revision, if later discovered and deemed illegal.

98. The approach adopted in the Model Law is a prohibition in principle of restrictive agreements. In consequence, when practices fall within the scope of

possible elements for articles 3 and 4, and are not prohibited outright, the possibility for their authorization exists. Notification also applies for Merger Control if this is provided for under possible elements for article 5 or under a separate article of the Law. It should be noted, however, that excessive provision for notification and registration in the law may be extremely burdensome for enterprises and for the responsible authorities. Therefore many laws requesting notification, such as in Spain, Sweden, or the European Community regulations, exempt or give "block exemptions" for specific practices, or for transactions below given thresholds. This will also be the case of Poland, under the proposed amendments to their law, presently under consideration by Parliament. In Sweden, block exemptions are similar to those in force within the European Community.

99. In seeking authorizations, enterprises would be required to notify the full details of intended agreements or arrangements to the Administering Authority. The particulars to be notified depend on the circumstances and are unlikely to be the same in every instance (see box 11). The information required could include, *inter alia*:

(a) The name(s) and registered address(es) of the party, or parties concerned;

(b) The names and the addresses of the directors and of the owner, or part owners;

(c) The names and addresses of the (major) shareholders, with details of their holdings;

(d) The names of any parent and interconnected enterprises;

(e) A description of the products, or services, concerned;

(f) The places of business of the enterprise(s), the nature of the business at each place, and the territory or territories covered by the activities of the enterprise(s);

(g) The date of commencement of any agreement;

(h) Its duration or, if it is terminable by notice, the period of notice required;

(i) The complete terms of the agreement, whether in writing or oral, in which oral terms would be reduced to writing.

100.   In seeking authorization, it is for the enterprises in question to demonstrate that the intended agreement will not have the effects proscribed by the law, or that it is not in contradiction with the objectives of the law. With regard to authorization in respect of behaviour falling under possible elements for article 5, information supplied in notifications of mergers should include, for example, the share of the market, total assets, total annual turnover and number of employees, including those of horizontally and vertically integrated or interconnected enterprises, in order to ascertain the market power of the enterprises concerned. Those enterprises falling in the category of "market dominating enterprises" (the specific criteria of which would need to be drawn up by the Administering Authority), and those which may as a result of such arrangements and practices meet those criteria, would have to notify the details, in full, to the Administering Authority. Box 11 indicates, for example, the type of information on relevant market to be supplied with notification and information to be supplied on relevant market in the case of a notification of a structural joint venture.

101.   In the Russian Federation, the Law has been amended recently. One of the principal amendments is introduction of the procedure that is similar to the "notification of agreements restricting competition" under the EC competition legislation in force. Thus, newly introduced Article 19.1 provides that economic entities intending to conclude an agreement to carry out coordinated actions are vested with right of submission of an application on verification of compliance of this agreement (concerted practices) with the provisions of the antimonopoly legislation to the antimonopoly bodies. The relevant antimonopoly body (i.e. MAP Russia or its regional office) issues an official opinion on compliance or non-compliance of the notified agreement (concerted actions) to antimonopoly legislation. In South Africa the period within which the enterprises must apply for authorization of agreements or arrangements falling within the scope of article 3 and 4 should be at least three months from the date of coming into force of the law. It is anticipated that enterprises would already have knowledge of the impending application of the law or of the coming into force of the law and they would make the necessary arrangements. It is considered that six months is more than sufficient to enable them to have prepared for notifications for authorization. The UK law provides for voluntary notification. Enterprises in Zambia can notify conduct that is not prohibited outright by the

---

Box 11

Notification: Information about the parties and the agreement

Identity of firms submitting the notification;

Information on the parties to the agreement and any corporate groups to which they belong;

Details of the agreements or arrangements notified, including any provisions which may restrict the parties in their freedom to take independent commercial decisions;

A non confidential summary which the Competition Authority can disclose on the *Official Gazette or on the Internet,* inviting comments from third parties;

Reasons why the Competition Authority should grant negative clearance or exemption;

Supporting documentation (e.g. annual reports and accounts for all parties for the last three years); Copies of in house or external long term market studies or planning documents;

Information on relevant market to be supplied with notification;

Identification of the relevant product market defined by the Competition Authority as comprising all those products and/or services which are regarded as interchangeable or substitutable by the consumer, by reason of the products' characteristics, their prices or their intended use;

Identification of the relevant geographical market defined by the Competition Authority as comprising the area in which the undertakings concerned are involved in the supply of products or services, in which the conditions of competition are sufficiently homogeneous and which can be distinguished from neighbouring areas because, in particular, conditions of competition are appreciably different in those areas; Position of the parties, competitors and customers in the relevant product market(s);

Market entry and potential competition in the product and geographical markets;

Information on relevant market for structural joint ventures;

Identification of relevant product and geographical markets as above, plus additional questions on the products or services directly or indirectly affected by the agreement;

Notified products or services which are close economic substitutes and more detailed questions on the geographical market;

Information on group members operating in the same markets;

Questions on parties, competitors and customers as above;

Questions on market entry and potential competition as above, plus additional details, e.g. on minimum viable scale for entry into the relevant product market(s).

Act under section 13. In Zambia the notification process is very similar to that of the authorization process. Notification can be made by any relevant party to the conduct or by their appointed representatives. Like the model law notification, it is entirely incumbent upon the notifying party/parties to demonstrate the public benefits outweigh any plausible anticompetitive detriment to the conduct. For details, see Annex III.

102. Notifications are allowed to stand for periods ranging from 3 to 5 years after which the Commission would review the notification vis-à-vis the public benefit attained. The Commission reserves the right to revoke a notification if the envisaged public benefits are not attained or when the anti competitive detriment outweigh public benefits. In Ukraine the law envisages authorisation if: (i) it does not result in the monopolisation of the whole market or its significant part or in the substantial restriction of competition on the whole market or in its significant part; (ii) the Cabinet of Ministers of Ukraine authorise concentration which was not permitted by the Antimonopoly Committee of Ukraine because the

concentration did not correspond with the conditions provided for by the law and if a positive effect produced by the concentration on the public interests outweighs negative consequences of the restriction of competition. However, authorisation may not be granted if restrictions of competition caused by the concentration are not necessary for attaining the purpose of the concentration or constitute a threat to the system of market economy[128].

II.   *Action by the Administering Authority*

1. Decision by the Administering Authority (within ... days/months of the receipt of full notification of all details), whether authorization is to be denied, granted or granted subject where appropriate to the fulfilment of conditions and obligations.

2. Periodical review procedure for authorizations granted every (...) months/years, with the possibility of extension, suspension, or the subjecting of an extension to the fulfilment of conditions and obligations.

103. The coming into force of agreements notified would depend on a number of factors. In the case of mergers and other acquisitions of control, the prior authorization of the Administering Authority in a given time frame before the coming into force of agreements should be envisaged. The same procedure could also be applied with respect to agreements and arrangements notified under articles 3 and 4 (e) to (f), but it could cause certain delays in business decisions. With regard to the latter, the agreements could perhaps come into force provisionally unless decided otherwise by the Administering Authority, within a given time frame.

104. Section II, paragraph 2, of this article provides for a review and suspension procedure for authorization granted. If authorizations are granted in particular economic circumstances, it is usually on the understanding that these circumstances are likely to continue. A review procedure is necessary, however, not only in cases where circumstances may have changed, but also where the possible adverse effects of the exemption were not predicted or foreseen at the time at which the authorization was given.

3. The possibility of withdrawing an authorization could be provided, for instance, if it comes to the attention of the Administering Authority that:

(a) The circumstances justifying the granting of the authorization have ceased to exist;

(b) The enterprises have failed to meet the conditions and obligations stipulated for the granting of the authorization;

(c) Information provided in seeking the authorization was false or misleading.

105. Section II, paragraph 3, provides for withdrawing an authorization when there has been a change of facts, or when a break of obligations, or an abuse of exemption has been committed. This also includes instances where the original decision was based on incorrect or deceitful information.

CHAPTER VI

Notification, examination and prohibition of mergers affecting concentrated markets

I.   *Notification*

Mergers, takeovers, joint ventures or other acquisitions of control, including interlocking directorships, whether of a horizontal, vertical, or conglomerate nature, should be notified when:

(i) At least one of the enterprises is established within the country; and

(ii) The resultant market share in the country, or any substantial part of it, relating to any product or service, is likely to create market power, especially in industries where there is a high degree of market concentration, where there are barriers to entry and where there is a lack of substitutes for a product supplied by firms whose conduct is under scrutiny.

II.   *Prohibition*

Mergers, takeovers, joint ventures or other acquisitions of control, including interlocking directorships, whether of a horizontal, vertical or conglomerate nature, should be prohibited when:

(i) The proposed transaction substantially increases the ability to exercise market power (e.g. to give the ability to a firm or group of firms acting jointly to profitably maintain prices above competitive levels for a significant period of time); and

(ii) The resultant market share in the country, or any substantial part of it, relating to any product or service, will result in a dominant firm or in a significant reduction of competition in a market dominated by very few firms.

III.   *Investigation procedures*

Provisions to allow investigation of mergers, takeovers, joint ventures or other acquisitions of control, including interlocking directorships, whether of a horizontal, vertical or conglomerate nature, which may harm competition could be set out in a regulation regarding concentrations.

In particular, no firm should, in the cases coming under the preceding subsections, effect a merger until the expiration of a (…) day waiting period from the date of the issuance of the receipt of the notification, unless the competition authority shortens the said period or extends it by an additional period of time not exceeding (…) days with the consent of the firms concerned, in accordance with the provisions of Possible Elements for Article 7 below. The authority could be empowered to demand documents and testimony from the parties and from enterprises in the affected relevant market or lines of commerce, with the parties losing additional time if their response is late.

If a full hearing before the competition authority or before a tribunal results in a finding against the transaction, acquisitions or mergers could be subject to being prevented or even undone whenever they are likely to lessen competition substantially in a line of commerce in the jurisdiction or in a significant part of the relevant market within the jurisdiction.

COMMENTARIES ON CHAPTER VI AND ALTERNATIVE APPROACHES IN EXISTING LEGISLATIONS

Notification, examination and prohibition of mergers affecting concentrated markets

I.   *Notification*

Mergers, takeovers, joint ventures, or other acquisitions of control, including interlocking directorships, whether of a horizontal, vertical, or a conglomerate nature, when:

(i) At least one of the enterprises is established within the country; and

(ii) The resultant market share in the country, or any substantial part of it, relating to any product or service, is likely to create market power, especially in industries where there is a high degree of market concentration, where there are barriers to entry and where there is a lack of substitutes for a product supplied by firms whose conduct is under scrutiny.

1.   Definitions

106.   Concentration of economic power occurs *inter alia* through mergers, takeovers, joint ventures and other acquisitions of control, such as interlocking directorates. A merger is a fusion between two or more enterprises "previously independent of one another" whereby the identity of one or more is lost and the result is a single enterprise. The takeover of one enterprise by another usually involves the purchase of all or a sufficient amount of the shares of another enterprise to enable it to exercise control, and it may take place without the consent of the former. A joint venture involves the formation of a separate enterprise by two or more enterprises.

107.   Such acquisitions of control might, in some cases, lead to a concentration of economic power which may be horizontal (for example, the acquisition of a competitor), vertical (for example, between enterprises at different stages of the manufacturing and distribution process), or conglomerate (involving different kinds of activities). In some cases such concentrations can be both horizontal and vertical, and the enterprises involved may originate in one or more countries[129]. Box 12 sums up the main reasons for instituting a merger control.

2.   Notification and criteria of notification

108.   Many States, in controlling mergers and other forms of acquisition of control, have established a system of notification prior to consummation of mergers such as in the United States and the European Union. Some countries have retained a mandatory system of notification after consummation of the merger and a few countries have submitted merger control only to a voluntary notification process. A list of the countries falling in these three categories can be found in a table in annex 2. For most countries, notification is mandatory only when the enterprises concerned have, or are likely to acquire, a certain level of concentration.

Box 12

Why institute a merger control?

Some countries with smaller markets believe that merger control is unnecessary because they do not want to impede restructuring of firms trying to obtain a "critical mass" which would enable them to be competitive in world markets. Others believe that having a "national champion" even abusing a monopoly position domestically might allow it to be competitive abroad in third markets. Two objections can be made to these views. First, it is often the case that monopolies enjoy their "monopoly rent" without becoming more competitive abroad, at the expense of domestic consumers and eventually of the development of the economy as a whole. Second, if the local market is open to competition from imports or FDI, the world market might be relevant for the merger control test, and the single domestic supplier might anyway be authorized to merge. It should also be noted that prohibiting a cartel, while being unable to act against the cartel members if they merge, is unwarranted. Moreover, by not having a merger control system, a host country deprives itself of the powers to challenge foreign mergers and acquisitions which might have adverse effects on the national territory.

As a rule, merger control aims at preventing the creation, through acquisitions or other structural combinations, of undertakings that will have the incentive and ability to exercise market power. Mergers that are in unusually concentrated markets, or that create firms with unusually high market shares, are thought more likely to affect competition.

Depending on the degree of experience of the competition authorities and varying from one jurisdiction to another, the test of legality of a merger is derived from the laws about dominance or restraints or a separate test is developed and phrased in terms of measures of the actual or potential effect on competition and the competitive process. In earlier versions of the Model Law, merger control was thus included in the possible elements for articles on the abuse of a dominant position.

Most merger control systems apply some form of market share test, either to guide further investigation or as a presumption about legality. Most systems specify procedures for pre notification to enforcement authorities in advance of larger, more important transactions, and special processes for pre expedited investigations, in order that problems can be identified and resolved before the restructuring is actually undertaken when the merger is consummated.

Merger control analysis incorporate the following aspects:

·   Relevant market definition in geographical or product terms;

·   Characterization of the products that actually or potentially compete;

·   Firms that might offer competition;

·   The relative shares and strategic importance of those firms with respect to the product markets;

·   The likelihood of new entry and the existence of effective barriers to new entry.

Tables in annex 3 give detailed examples of thresholds triggering the mandatory (*ex ante* and *ex post*) or voluntary notifications systems for a number of countries as well as indication about the whole merger control system of selected developed and developing countries and countries in transition. In Taiwan, Province of China, the merger regulation of the FTL was switched from prior approval to notification in the 2002 amendment. The notification threshold for the financial sector is 10 billion NT dollars (US$ 2.9 billion) and the amount of previous year's sale of the business to be acquired should exceed US$ 290 million. For the non-financial sector, the total amount of sales from the previous year exceeds NT$ 2 billion (US$ 580 million) and the acquired business exceeds NT$ 0.39 billion (US$ 115 million). In Armenia, Article 9 sets out the thresholds for notification: if the total gross income of the parties to the concentration has been equivalent to more than US$ 4 million equivalent in AMD in the year preceding the creation of the concentration, or if at least one of the parties to the concentration is entered on the register of economic entities with dominant position on the given commodity market.

109. Furthermore, the Armenian Law (Art 10) regulates concentrations as follows:

(i) Any concentration leading to a dominant position shall be prohibited except when the concentration fosters the development of competition on the given commodity market.

(ii) The concentration shall be permitted on the basis of a decision made pursuant to a procedure laid down in the present law.

In Chile, there is no obligation of pre-notification of acts of concentration, acquisitions or mergers. In practice, merger control is effected by the Central Preventive Commission, which is empowered to deal with inquiries about existing acts or contracts that might infringe the provisions of the law. For its part, the Resolutive Commission is entitled to consider mergers that alter or limit competition, as well as takeovers and acquisitions (Resolution No. 639 of 23 January 2002). In the Zambian legislation, merger control regulation under Section 8 of the Act applies to all mergers in the economy that involve the acquisition or the establishment of control over a significant interest in the whole or a part of a business of a competitor, supplier, customer or other person[130].

110. In the Indian Competition Act 2002, the acquisition of one or more enterprises by one or more persons or merger or the amalgamation of enterprises shall be a combination of such enterprises and persons. The Act makes it voluntary for the parties to notify their proposed agreement or combination to the Competition Commission. Such voluntary notification is applicable only if the aggregate assets of the combining parties have a value in excess of specified limits. Separate asset limits have been specified for groups of enterprises defined based on cross shareholding or interlocking directorships. Separate asset limits have been specified when global (worldwide) assets are involved.

Combinations which causes or are likely to cause an appreciable adverse effect on competition within the relevant market in India are considered to be void. The Act specifies in (section. 20 (4)) taking cognizance of the several factors for the purpose of determining whether a combination would have the effect of or is likely to have an appreciable adverse effect on competition in the relevant markets[131].

The Zambian legislation does not define "merger", "acquisition", "joint-control", or "joint-venture", or the notification procedure for mergers and acquisitions. However, merger guidelines provide relevant information to the parties, and pre-notification is a mandatory requirement. The assessment of mergers or takeovers by the Commission focuses on the question of whether a proposed transaction is likely to prevent, distort or lessen competition in a relevant market. Some mergers and takeovers are, however, prohibited outright by the Act. Others can be authorized by the Commission and others are legal and do not need to be authorized. It is an offence under the Act to effect a merger between two or more enterprises engaged in manufacturing or distributing substantially similar goods or services (horizontal mergers). The Act sets two thresholds, one to deal with the situation of unilateral market power (i.e. single firm dominance) and the other to deal with the situation of concentrated markets, where they may be combined or oligopoly market power[132]. The thresholds are set so that the Commission would look at mergers which have:

· Unilateral market power: the merged firm has more than 50% of the market; and

· Combined market power: a dominant undertaking which together with more than two independent undertakings have more than 50% of the market.

111. In Zimbabwe notification of merger must be made within thirty days of the conclusion of the merger agreement between the merging parties or of the acquisition by any one of the parties to that merger or a controlling interest in another.

112. The main indicators used for examining such concentration of economic power are market shares, total annual turnover, number of employees and total assets. The other factors, including the general market structure, the existing degree of market concentration, barriers to entry and the competitive position of other enterprises in the relevant market, as well as the advantages currently enjoyed and to be gained by the acquisition, are also taken into account in assessing the effects of an acquisition. It is important to note that authorization schemes must not be interpreted as to discourage firms from undertaking pro competitive activities[133]. In the European Union, the obligation to notify a concentration is based on the worldwide, community wide or national aggregate turnover of the concerned undertaking.

113.   For example, in 1989 the European Union adopted a comprehensive system of merger control through Regulation No. 4064/89. This regulation was extensively modified in 1997, "et fait l'objet d'une nouvelle révision prévue pour entrer en vigueur au 1er mai 2004". The Merger Regulation is based on the principle of a "one stop shop": once a transaction has triggered the application of the European Competition Authority powers (e.g. the European Commission through its Directorate General for Competition), the national competition authorities of the member States are precluded from applying their own competition laws to the transaction (except in very limited circumstances). The application of this principle is aimed at strengthening the firms' certainty with regard to international transactions (which otherwise could fall under the review of multiple national merger control authorities). This principle of the "one stop shop" has been strengthened by the modification, in an attempt to reduce the need for the business community to make multiple applications for clearance with national merger regulators[134,135].

114.   Until 1 March 1998, the regulation required the notification of all mergers or acquisitions between firms with a combined turnover of 5 billion euros, each having a turnover of at least 250 million euros in the EC, unless each of the parties achieves more than two thirds of its aggregate Community wide turnover in one and the same member State. Since 1 March 1998, the Merger Regulation has also applied to smaller concentrations which have a significant impact in at least three member States. The Regulation catches the concentrations where the aggregate Community wide turnover of the parties exceeds 2.5 billion euros, and where the Community wide turnover of each of at least two parties exceeds 100 million euros and where in each of at least three member States, the aggregate turnover of all the parties exceeds 100 million euros and in each of the three just mentioned member States the turnover of each of at least two parties exceeds 25 million euros, unless each of the parties achieves more than two thirds of its aggregate Community wide turnover in one and the same member State.

115.   Such transactions have to be notified, and halted for up to four months if investigated. It is rare to see corporations failing to comply with the obligation to notify: for instance in the EU, over 10 years of practice of enforcement, the Commission first imposed a financial penalty on an enterprise for failure to notify a

concentration in time only in 1998[136]. Mergers which do not reach the threshold indicated may still be subject to control by the national authorities of the member States once they exceed the jurisdictional thresholds defined by the domestic legislation. Also, there are exceptions which may, in any case, bring a merger back within a member State's ambit[137], or, alternatively, bring an application which is subject to one or more national controls back within the Community ambit[138].

In the current EC practice, the normal waiting period ("Phase I deadline" is one month and is automatically extended to 6 weeks if the merging parties offer commitments ("remedies") or if Member States request that the case be referred to them. The waiting period can be extended unilaterally by the Commission (i.e. without the consent of the merging parties) where it considers that the case raises serious doubts as to its compatibility with the common market for an additional 4 months (so-called "Phase II"). The European Commission can grant derogations from the suspensive effect, i.e. it can allow merging parties to partially or fully implement their transaction (See Articles 7 and 10 ECMR). Note that some changes to the EC system of deadlines, including new elements of flexibility, are laid down in the Commission's proposal for a new Merger Regulation (Article 10 thereof). The EC Merger control system also provides for a possibility to order the de-merger of undertakings (see Article 8(4) ECMR). This provision will be further clarified and complemented in the proposed new Merger Regulation (Article 8(4) and 8(5) thereof).

3.   Types of concentrations

116.   Horizontal acquisitions are clearly the type of activity which contributes most directly to concentration of economic power and which is likely to lead to a dominant position of market power, thereby reducing or eliminating competition[139]. This is why restrictive business practices legislation in many developed and developing countries applies strict control to the merging or integration of competitors. In fact, one of the primary purposes of anti monopoly legislation has been to control the growth of monopoly power, which is often created as a direct result of integration of competitors into a single unit. Horizontal acquisitions of control are not limited to mergers but may also be effected through takeovers, joint ventures or interlocking directorates. Horizontal acquisition of control, even between small enterprises, while not necessarily adversely affecting competition in

the market, may nonetheless create conditions which can trigger further concentration of economic power and oligopoly.

117. Where the acquisition of control is through the establishment of a joint venture, the first consideration should be to establish whether the agreement is of the type proscribed by the possible elements for article 3, and involving market allocation arrangements or likely to lead to allocation of sales and production.

118. Vertical acquisitions of control involve enterprises at different stages in the production and distribution process, and may entail a number of adverse effects. For example, a supplying enterprise which merges or acquires a customer enterprise can extend its control over the market by foreclosing an actual or potential outlet for the products of its competitors. By acquiring a supplier, a customer can similarly limit access to supplies of its competitors.

119. Conglomerate acquisitions which neither constitute the bringing together of competitors nor have a vertical connection (i.e. forms of diversification into totally unrelated fields) are more difficult to deal with, since it could appear ostensibly that the structure of competition in relevant markets would not change. The most important element to be considered in this context is the additional financial strength which the arrangement will give to the parties concerned. A considerable increase in the financial strength of the combined enterprise could provide for a wider scope of action and leverage vis à vis competitors or potential competitors of both the acquired and the acquiring enterprise and especially if one or both are in a dominant position of market power. Some range or portfolio effects of brands may also come into play and create a restriction on competition, particularly in the relations between suppliers and distributors.

120. Cross frontier acquisitions of control. Mergers, takeovers or other acquisitions of control involving transnational corporations should be subject to some kind of scrutiny in all countries where the corporation operates, since such acquisitions of control, irrespective of whether they take place solely within a country or abroad, might have direct or indirect effects on the operations of other units of the economic entity, including the elimination of a potential competitor. In Taiwan, Province of China, the TFTC considers the following factors when determining jurisdiction in extraterritorial merger cases:

(1) The relative weight of the merger's effects on the relevant domestic and foreign markets;

(2) The nationalities, residence, and main business places of the combining enterprises;

(3) The explicitness of the intent to affect market competition and the foreseeability of effects on market competition;

(4) The likelihood of creating conflicts with the laws or policies of the home countries of the combining enterprises;

(5) The feasibility of enforcing administrative dispositions;

(6) The effect of enforcement on the foreign enterprises;

(7) Rules of international conventions and treaties, or, regulations of international organizations; and

(8) Other factors deemed important by the TFTC.

If none of the combining enterprises in an extraterritorial merger case has production or service facilities, distributors, agents, or other substantive sales channels within the territorial domain of Taiwan, Province of China, jurisdiction is not exercised[140].

121. Australia amended its legislation to strengthen and improve the effectiveness of the Trade Practices Act, 1986 to cover overseas mergers of foreign corporations with subsidiaries in Australia. Subsection 50 (A) (1) provides that the Tribunal may, on the application of the Minister, the Commission or any other person, make declaration that the person who, as a consequence of an acquisition outside Australia, obtains a controlling interest (defined by subsection 50 (A) (8)) in one or more corporations, would or would be likely to have the effect of substantially lessening competition in a substantial market for goods and services, and that the acquisition will not result in a net public benefit. The term "substantial market for goods and services" is used to make it clear that the provision applies only to markets of a similar magnitude to those to which section 50 applies[141].

122. Interesting examples of action against international mergers taking place outside the national borders, but

having effects in the national territory, are provided by the Federal Cartel Office of Germany, in the Bayer/Firestone, and in the Phillip Morris/Rothmans mergers case[142]. or, with respect to the French authorities, in the Boeing/Jeppesen case[143]. It is to be noted that there are several cases of restrictive business practices which have had effects in various countries and, hence, various national authorities have dealt with them. For instance, in 1998, 14 merger cases of an EC dimension involving several EU national authorities were notified to the European Commission. Particularly prominent are the Gillette/Wilkinson and the Boeing/McDonnell Douglas Mergers[144].

123. An interlocking directorship is a situation where a person is a member of the board of directors of two or more enterprises or the representatives of two or more enterprises meet on the board of directors of one firm. This would include interlocking directorship among parent companies, a parent of one enterprise and a subsidiary of another parent or between subsidiaries of different parents. Generally, financial tie ups and common ownership of stocks give rise to such situations.

124. Interlocking directorships can affect competition in a number of ways. They can lead to administrative control whereby decisions regarding investment and production can in effect lead to the formation of common strategies among enterprises on prices, market allocations and other concerted activities of the type discussed in article 3. Interlocking directorates at the vertical level can result in vertical integration of activities, such as, for example, between suppliers and customers, discourage expansion into competitive areas, and lead to reciprocal arrangements among them. Links between directorates of financial enterprises and non financial enterprises can result in discriminatory conditions of financing for competitors and act as catalysts for vertical horizontal or conglomerate acquisitions of control[145].

125. It is important to note that interlocking directorship can be used as a means of circumventing any well constructed and rigorously applied legislation in the area of restrictive business practices, if it is not effectively controlled[146]. Therefore, States may wish to consider mandatory notification of interlocking directorates and prior approval thereof, irrespective of whether the interlocking is among competitors, vertical or conglomerate.

CHAPTER VII

The relationship between competition authority and regulatory bodies, including sectoral regulators

I.   *Advocacy role of competition authorities with regard to regulation and regulatory reform*

126. An economic and administrative regulation issued by executive authorities, local self-government bodies or bodies enjoying a governmental delegation, especially when such a regulation relates to sectors operated by infrastructure industries, should be subjected to a transparent review process by competition authorities prior to its adoption. Such should in particular be the case if this regulation limits the independence and liberty of action of economic agents and/or if it creates discriminatory or, on the contrary, favourable conditions for the activity of particular firms – public or private – and/or if it results or may result in a restriction of competition and/or infringement of the interests of firms or citizens.

127. In particular, regulatory barriers to competition incorporated in the economic and administrative regulation, should be assessed by competition authorities from an economic perspective, including for general-interest reasons.

II.   *Definition of regulation*

128. The term " regulation " refers to the various instruments by which Governments impose requirements on enterprises and citizens. It thus embraces laws, formal and informal orders, administrative guidance and subordinate rules issued by all levels of government, as well as rules issued by non-governmental or professional self-regulatory bodies to which Governments have delegated regulatory powers.

III.   *Definition of regulatory barriers to competition*

129. As differentiated from structural and strategic barriers to entry, regulatory barriers to entry result from acts issued or acts performed by governmental executive authorities, by local self-government bodies, and by non-governmental or self-regulatory bodies to which Governments have delegated regulatory powers. They include administrative barriers to entry into a market, exclusive rights, certificates, licences and other permits

for starting business operations.

IV. *Protection of general interest*

130. Irrespective of their nature and of their relation to the market, some service activities performed by private or government-owned firms can be considered by Governments to be of general interest. Accordingly, the providers of services of general interest can be subject to specific obligations, such as guaranteeing universal access to various types of quality services at affordable prices. These obligations, which belong to the area of social and economic regulation, should be set out in a transparent manner.

131. The broad and commonly admitted purpose of competition policy is to minimize the economic inefficiencies created in markets by anti-competitive behaviours[147]. Competition policy consists not only of competition law enforcement, but also of trade liberalization and deregulation in the interest of consumers' welfare. Competition law and policy are intended to regulate non-competitive behaviours by firms, whereas deregulation is aimed at minimizing market-distorting government intervention. The possible elements for article 5 sets out four elements of definitions respectively regarding the advocacy role of competition agencies, the definitions of regulation and regulatory barriers to competition and the protection of general interest. In India for example under Sec. 49 of the Indian Competition Act 2002: In formulating a policy on competition (including review of laws to competition), the Central Government may make a reference to the Commission for its opinion on possible effect of such policy on competition and on receipt of such a reference, the Commission shall, within sixty days of making such a reference, give its opinion to the Central Government, which may thereafter formulate the policy as it deems fit. The opinion given by the Competition Commission shall not be binding on the Central Government while formulating the policy. The Commission shall take suitable measures for the promotion of competition advocacy, creating awareness and imparting training about competition issues.

132. An economic and administrative regulation issued by executive authorities, local self-government bodies or bodies enjoying a governmental delegation, especially when such a regulation relates to sectors operated by infrastructure industries, should be subjected to a transparent review process by competition authorities prior to its adoption. Such should in particular be the case if this regulation limits the independence and liberty of action of economic agents and/or if it creates discriminatory or, on the contrary, favourable conditions for the activity of particular firms – public or private – and/or if it results or may result in a restriction of competition and/or infringement of the interests of firms or citizens.

133. In particular, regulatory barriers to competition incorporated in the economic and administrative regulation, should be assessed by competition authorities from an economic perspective, including for general-interest reasons.

Elements related to the proposed article raise two issues, which need to be treated separately.

1. Why do Governments pay particular attention to the performance of certain economic activities?

134. Governments tend to develop extensive and comprehensive sectoral rules applying in particular to major infrastructure service industries. Such industries, also referred to as "public utilities" or "public services", include activities where consumption is indispensable for the development of modern ways of life or which provide essential inputs to many parts of a nation's economy, such as electricity, gas, water production and distribution, solid waste management, telecommunications, cable television, mail distribution and public transportation (by air, road or rail)[148].

135. There are four main reasons why Governments attach great importance to infrastructure service industries both in developed and developing countries and in countries in transition. Governmental prescription of their functioning distinguishes them in four ways from common and traditionally competitive sectors of the economy: by control of entry, price fixing or capping, and the quality and the conditions of service prescriptions.

136. The first reason is that these industries are fundamental to the performance of the economy as providers of inputs for all other sectors of activity. The conditions of their operations and efficiency may determine not only the general productivity and level of competitiveness of a country but also social order and even political stability if consumers express general

dissatisfaction. It follows from the essential nature of these industries that they often have public or universal service obligations, which means that the firms – public or private – are required to provide a particular service even when it is not economic for them to do so. Thus, infrastructure service industries may not be competitive where there are regulatory restraints on competition in the activity concerned. Restraints are imposed on competition for various reasons, including, most commonly, to permit a firm to find a source of revenue to fund mandated non-commercial activities and services. For example, a national postal operator often has protection from competition in standard letter mail, which is justified on the ground that it is necessary in order to protect the cross-subsidization of letter delivery in high-cost areas such as rural areas. The result is that reform of these sectors which are essential to a country's activity and are protected from competition for social and political reasons is often highly politicized.

137.   The second reason is that the activities of these infrastructure service industries can be performed only by a very small number of operators at the national level; in other words, most governmental entities, such as local government units (e.g. cities, provinces, federated States), are faced with a very strong and concentrated bargaining power. In many countries central or local governments have decided to assume direct ownership of infrastructure service industries.

138.   The third reason, which has a bearing on regulation and competition, is that these industries often involve considerable barriers to entry or exit, such as sunk costs which are unrecoverable once they have been committed. In particular, the sequence of operations is of importance with respect to governmental regulation: often, major investments have first to be made in a situation where investors commit to the market and second rents or revenues will arrive over a period of several years. This means that, to attract voluntary private investment, the framers of the regulatory regime have to make it credible and predictable. This concern for credibility is often shared by Treasury policy-makers. Creating credibility and predictability is one of the basic tasks of a regulator.

139.   The fourth, and final, reason why Governments attach great importance to infrastructure service industries derives from supply, costs and demand effects, owing to the fact that such a sector is not made up of a single homogeneous activity but comprehends a number of separate components. Some parts of these components

cannot sustain competition, generally because of the presence of economies of scale, a situation in which a single firm in a defined area can meet market demand more efficiently than any combination of two or more firms. This component which cannot sustain competition usually requires the use of a privilege, or exclusive right of use of some public good which is owned by the Government and has to be given or lent by it. An infrastructure service industry may also not be able to sustain competition owing to the presence of "network effects" or "demand-side economies of scale" – that is, when the demand for a firm's services increases with the consumption of those services[149].

140.   From the particular perspective of developing countries, it should be stressed that market structure often raises serious concerns about enhancing efficiency through regulatory reform and opening regulated industries to competition.

141.   For instance, it has been recently and repeatedly observed that the process of reform utilities in South America has not considered market evaluation prior to privatization of public assets in infrastructure industries. The regulated and unregulated activities constituting the market structure were generally undifferentiated, owing to earlier government intervention[150]. Asian developing countries are having a similar experience as regulatory review processes are initiated. For instance, a representative of Papua New Guinea recently stressed the fact that regulatory restrictions imposed by government regulation or government ownership are an impediment to competition. In Papua New Guinea, the existing regulations were put in place when there was greater confidence in them, but less appreciation of their costs:

"Examples include legislated monopolies for public utilities, statutory marketing arrangements for many agricultural products and licensing arrangements for various occupations and professions. The Central Agencies Working Group will carry out a review of barriers to entry... Structural reforms may be required to dismantle excessive market power that may impede the introduction of effective competition. In order for privatization to achieve its objective of improved efficiency, it is important for these structural reforms to be carried out first. This will require structural separation in two areas: the separation of regulatory and commercial functions and the separation of natural monopolies and potentially competitive activities"[151].

142.   The examples given by the official from Papua New Guinea show that developing countries' concerns are indeed very close to those of developed countries. Efficient regulation in developed countries traditionally distinguishes between network segments which are non-potentially competitive and segments of production and retailing which are generally considered to be natural monopolies and non-potentially competitive. Potentially competitive segments comprise, for instance, long distance in telecommunications, generation in electricity and transportation in railways. Non-potentially competitive segments include the transmission grid in electricity, the tracks in railways and the local loop in telecom communications; they often remain regulated after competition of the regulatory reform process. It is clear that the lack of effective separation gives market power to firms operating network infrastructures. Such power, exercised at the expense of other operators and consumers, should be kept under control.

2.   What should be the role of competition agencies with respect to regulation?

143.   From a market structure point of view, the competition authorities should be consulted when a process of regulatory reform is being undertaken as a part of a privatization program. They should be given legal powers to impose divestiture measures on existing monopolies or to control or prohibit mergers that undermine competitive market structures. If they are not given such powers, for instance because of lack of human resources, it should be made possible for them to suggest divestiture measures or merger controls to an executive authority that has those powers[152]. Nevertheless, it is clear that the dominant pattern of distribution of roles between competition agencies and regulatory agencies is rarely one whereby competition authorities simply replace regulatory agencies.

144.   However, it is interesting to look at the present relationship between competition authorities and sectoral regulators in most member countries of the Organisation for Economic Co-operation and Development (OECD). A study of these relationships shows that the competitive process can be appropriately stimulated by the intervention of competition authorities when firms in a regulated sector abuse their privileges to the detriment of consumer interests and the efficiency of firms that use their regulated services. The experience of deregulation in the most developed countries gives rise

to four main observations:

145.   First, there are specific regulatory regimes in many sectors in OECD and developing countries; they are particularly common in sectors such as telecommunications, electricity, railways and natural gas. However, such regimes are also found in radio and television broadcasting, civil aviation, cable television, ocean shipping, pharmaceuticals, radioactive minerals, alcoholic beverages, insurance, banking, inter-city bus transportation and trucking, and water distribution, as well as in numerous other sectors.

146.   Second, there is no unique model for the relationship between sector-specific regulators and competition authorities either across countries or sometimes even within a country. However, one particular model – the mandate-driven division of labour approach – appears to be somewhat more common than others. It is clear, at least, that sectoral regulators should be separated from regulated firms or entities and should assume obligations regarding accountability and independence from the executive branch of government. Also, institutional changes should be effected in order to guarantee their independence. As recently and repeatedly pointed out by officials from the Republic of Korea, since sector-specific enforcement of competition law may be characterized by inconsistencies, regulators should first consult and coordinate with competition authorities[153].

147.   Third, in countries that deregulated somewhat earlier than others, a rather pragmatic approach seems to have emerged, which differs empirically from one sector to another. Countries liberalizing somewhat later appear to have followed a more systematic approach.

148.   Finally, there is a good deal of variation across countries in the terminology used. Some countries make a distinction between technical regulation, economic regulation and competition law enforcement. But sometimes, "competition policy" seems to be included in "economic regulation". In some OECD countries, there also appears to be a tendency to use "economic regulation" and "technical regulation" interchangeably.

II.   *Definition of Regulation*

The term "regulation" refers to the various instruments by which Governments impose requirements on enterprises and citizens. It thus embraces laws, formal and informal orders, administrative guidance and subordinate rules issued by all levels of government, as well as rules issued by non-governmental or professional self-regulatory bodies to which Governments have delegated regulatory powers.

Regulation can pursue different types of objectives. Economic regulation, social regulation and administrative regulation are among the three main categories of government intervention which may have a bearing on the market. Economic regulation includes government requirements which intervene directly in market decisions, such as pricing, competition, and market entry or exit. Social regulation includes government requirements which protect public interests such as health, safety, the environment and social cohesion. Administrative regulation includes paperwork and formalities through which Governments collect information and intervene in individual economic decisions. In designing their regulation principles, competition authorities should be given opportunities to assess potential effects of the envisioned regulation in light of efficiency principles (see box 13).

III.   *Definition of regulatory barriers to competition*

149.   As differentiated from structural and strategic barriers to entry, regulatory barriers to entry result from acts issued or acts performed by governmental executive authorities, by local self-government bodies, and by non-governmental or self-regulatory bodies to which Governments have delegated regulatory powers. They include administrative barriers to entry into a market, exclusive rights, certificates, licences and other permits for starting business operations.

Regulatory barriers to competition consist of measures taken by state administrations (e.g. central or federal government, local government) or by bodies enjoying a governmental delegation, which prevent or hamper effective competition and which in the final analysis lead to a loss in welfare. Such measures are to be found in as diverse activities as telecommunications, financial services (banking and insurance), professional business services (accounting, lawyers, architects etc.), and the energy sector (electricity, gas), as evidenced by

---

Box 13

Efficient regulation principles for the removal of regulatory barriers to competition

Efficient regulation principles should be built into domestic regulatory processes for social and economic regulations as well as administrative formalities. They are particularly useful with regard to regional economic integration. Such principles include:

- *Non-discrimination, especially in respect of standards.* There should be equality of competitive opportunities between like products and services, irrespective of countries of origin. Performance-based rather than design standards should be used as the basis of technical regulation; taxes or tradable permits should be used in place of regulation. When appropriate and feasible, internationally harmonized measures should be used as the basis of domestic regulations.
- *Recognition of equivalence of other countries' regulatory measures.* When internationally harmonized measures are not possible, necessary or desirable, the negative effects on cross-country markets caused by disparities in regulation and duplicative conformity assessment systems can be reduced by recognizing the equivalence of trading partners' regulatory measures or the results of conformity assessment carried out in other countries.

Source : OECD, *Report on Regulatory Reform,* Paris, 1997.

an abundant literature[154]. These measures, which can negatively affect market entry, market exit and market operation, take a wide variety of forms, such as:

– Restraints on competition, i.e. by introducing uncommon norms and standards amounting to barriers to market entry or by preventing foreign firms from competing in national market;

– Elimination or exclusion from competition through exemption of certain activities from the scope and coverage of competition laws[155];

– Creation of distortions to competition, such as artificial executive interventions changing the competitive positions of certain firms (through arbitrary public procurement policy decisions, for instance).

150. Regulatory barriers to competition not only relate to market entry but also can prevent market exit from happening, for instance through public subsidization or the granting or prolongation of monopoly rights. In addition, they can make it harder for resources to be allocated from one sector or market segment to another. They can be considered barriers to mobility which prevents resources from being transferred into more efficient sectors or segments, and which in the end will reduce allocative efficiency.

IV. *Protection of general interest*

151. Irrespective of their nature and of their relation to the market, some service activities performed by private or government-owned firms can be considered by Governments to be of general interest. Accordingly, the providers of services of general interest can be subject to specific obligations, such as guaranteeing universal access to various types of quality services at affordable prices. These obligations, which belong to the area of social and economic regulation, should be set out in a transparent manner.

152. In the design of their regulatory schemes, several countries have defined a necessity of preserving a general or public "interest" which is generally delegated to different types of public authorities or entities. Among these entities, ithe units of local government can be involved in the market functioning in several respects. Therefore, the interaction of regulation and competition should include an analysis of the role of local governments[156].

1. How the protection of the "general interest" relates to regulation?

153. The protection of general interest is generally the most frequent feature sustaining regulation. Where it has been recognized that free competition cannot or does not provide sufficient results with regard to the quality, regularity, affordability, territorial coverage and security of services of general interest, generally performed by infrastructure service industries, Governments should be allowed to impose non-discriminatory and transparent regulations on all operators in the market, compelling them to meet certain standards for as long as they are operating n the market. Such a competition-friendly way of ensuring services of general economic interest has been the subject of in-depth research and study in the European Union, in connection with legislation designed to liberalize various sectors of the economy[157].

2. Regulation, competition and local governments

154. In States which are characterized by a strong federal division of powers between the Federal State Authorities and Federated States or Regional Authorities, local regulations are often invoked by operators as a defense shielding them from the enforceability of competition Law. Firms may either seek special Regulations or even Subsidies from Local State Authorities. In the Regulatory Reform exercise which was conducted in several OECD member States, such as Spain or Mexico, it has been often stressed that such local regulations impeding interstate trade are indeed submitted to control of Federal Competition Authorities[158]. The European Union Treaty submits under certain conditions both enterprises enjoying special and / or exclusive rights and State and Regional or Local Subsidies to the monitoring control of the E.U. Commission in charge of the enforcement of Competition rules. This system is worth studying because it addresses several issues pertaining to regional economic integration and the interaction of regulation and competition (see box 14).

Box 14

The submission of regional authorities to competition review: the European Union toolkit

The European Union is a recent creation, incorporated in the Maastricht Treaty of February 7, 1992. But the major European competition rules provisions were created much longer ago by the Treaty of Rome of March 25, 1957, creating the European Economic Community, now called the European Community which is a constituent part of the European Union. The Maastricht Treaty has been modified by the Treaty of Amsterdam of October 2, 1997, and most recently by the Treaty of Nice of 26 February 2001 which entered into force on 1 Februray 2003 and resulted in the recent renumbering of all the original provisions of the Treaty of Rome, including those related to competition.

In 1957, the Constitution of the E.C., the Treaty of Rome, stated in its article 3 (g) that the Community had to create and maintain "a system ensuring that competition in the common market is not distorted". And the explicit reference to competition rules in the E.C. Constitution has had a significant and long standing effect on the decision making process of the Commission, the Court of First Instance (the Appeal Tribunal for decisions of the Commission, notably in the field of competition law enforcement) and the European Court of Justice (the European Supreme Court), which have often interpreted the competition rules from that starting point of Article 3(g) in the light of all provisions of the European Treaty.

Today, the competition rules of the E.U. are thus contained in the provisions of Articles 31 (ex-Article 37), and 81 to 90 (ex-Articles 85 to 94). And we will see later that, as far as regulation and deregulation are concerned, one should more especially pay due attention to Articles 86 and 95.

Market integration principles

Articles 31 and 49 to 55 are often forgotten in the presentation of the Competition principles of the E.U., but as far as Market integration, it must be considered as complementary to the actual provisions on competition included in Articles 81 to 90 to create a competitive environment within the European Single Market. Articles 31 and 49 to 55 relate respectively to national monopolies regulations and to the free movement services and national regulations which restrain the free movement of these services: a manufacturing or an infrastructure services firm may find that it cannot compete on a relevant market for numerous reasons quite apart from the actual anti-competitive behavior of private or public corporations, for instance because of a national regulation which discriminates or forecloses the national market to non-national operators. Furthermore, as public procurement represents as much as about 11% of the E.U. GDP, upon the initiative of the Commission, the Council of Ministers of the Union has also designed a series of "Directives" aiming at the public procurement policies of Member States which may discriminate against firms established in other Member States and designed to open up these procurement policies to pan-European competitive tendering.

Articles 81 to 90 of the Treaty of Rome are better known than most of the other Articles of that Treaty although most people pay more attention to Articles 81 and 82 containing the antitrust provisions respectively prohibiting anti-competitive agreements and abuses of a dominant position and which are the European equivalent of Sections 1 and 2 of the U.S. Sherman Act. These Articles 81 and 82 are chiefly applied to anti-competitive behaviours of private firms.

Infrastructure regulation

As far as the relationships between competition policy and sectoral regulation is concerned, Article 82 enforced in connection with Article 86 has been used to tackle anti-competitive behaviours of firms – both privately and publicly owned – which operate in infrastructure service industries. Article 86 can been seen as a key instrument for strengthening the Single Market integration in the infrastructure service industries. Within the European Union, the model of regulation is chiefly governed by the provisions of Article 86 (ex-Article 90) of the modified Rome Treaty which define the principle of liberalization. The Article 86 is enforced by the Commission. Its provisions extend the enforcement of the E.U. Competition law to public undertakings as well as undertakings enjoying special or exclusive rights i.e. enjoying a monopoly status to perform a service activity in the "general economic interest": for these firms, be they public or private, Member States may not give rights or maintain regulations ("measures" in the E.U. legal formulation) which could impede the competition rules vested in the Treaty. The purpose of the competition-based Article 86 principle is to strengthen the European economic integration by removing the rights granted to monopolies as far as this removal does not run against Member States and the European Community commitments to services of a general economic interest.

Thereby, the E.U. Commission in charge of the Treaty enforcement has adopted in the last decade a number of Decisions and Regulations removing legal entry barriers across Member States for infrastructure service industries while extending competition rules enforcement to the firms operating in these sectors, as far as the general interests were not harmed.

To define what is meant by "general interest", the Commission has explained in its Guidelines from 1996, that this extension of competition rules would not run against obligations of public service that may be imposed by the public authorities on the entities – public or private – that perform the services for the sake of protection of economic and social cohesion, of the environment, of the planning and promotion of consumers interests and land use.

Furthermore, the principle of opening to competition or "liberalization" rooted in Article 86 is complemented by the principle of "harmonization" which lies in the long and complex procedural Article 95 (ex-Article 100-A) of the Treaty. The provisions of Article 95 aim at bringing together the Laws of the Member States or, in other words, to "harmonize" theses Laws by setting out procedures by which both the Commission and the Council of Ministers of the E.U. can adopt "Directives" to impose to Member States the removal of barriers to the further construction and integration of the Internal Market.

More specifically, for infrastructure service industries, this principle of harmonization implies that the Commission can propose to the Council of Ministers the conditions by which Member States will have to align or "harmonize" their sector-specific regulatory regimes to further integrate the European Market. Whereas the enforcement of the Article 86 seems to be more reactive *ex-post* to individual behaviors of States or firms enjoying special or exclusive rights on a case-by-case basis, the enforcement of Article 95 is more proactive ex-ante: the use of Article 95 aims at organizing a harmonized framework of regulatory rules to ensure business and investors security within the Internal Market as well as to effectively unify the Single Market for firms operating in the field of infrastructure service industries.

Public subsidies

And finally, the fact that Articles 87 to 89 provide the Commission with powers to deal with State Aids that could distort competition in the European Single Market should be stressed. It is a unique feature in the World of Competition Agencies and Regulators to provide a body with such a powerful tool to prohibit States from distorting the rule of competition. Even if exceptions are acceptable they are publicly and transparently monitored by the Commission which has developed an important case law on the matter.

Article 87(1) provides that: "save as otherwise provided in this Treaty, any aid granted by a Member State or through State resources in any form whatsoever which distorts or threatens to distort competition by favouring certain undertakings or the production of certain goods shall, in so far as it affects trade between Member States, be incompatible with the Common Market". But Article 87(3) nevertheless provides the Commission with the discretion to analyze and authorize other aids, for instance to promote economic development of areas where the standard of living is abnormally low or where there is serious unemployment, or to promote the execution of an important project of Common European interest or to remedy a serious disturbance in the economy of a Member State, just as Article 87(2) specifies that aids having a social character granted to individual consumers, aids to make good the damage caused by national disasters or exceptional circumstances are compatible with the Common Market.

With regard to State aids, Article 89 is also of interest because it gives an insight into procedural matters which will be visited in some details in the following section. Under this Article, the Commission may adopt a decision – published to the Official journal of the EU – that a State Aid which is incompatible with the Common Market has to be abolished or altered. If the Member State does not comply with this decision within the stated time, the Commission, or another Member State may take the matter to the European Court of Justice following a simplified and accelerated procedure. Then repayments of unduly attributed aids can be demanded. Furthermore, prior to the attribution of aids, plans to grant or alter aids must be notified to the Commission in sufficient time to enable it to submit its comments and aids may not be implemented until the Commission has reached a decision. In other words, the Treaty of Rome has had to organise a deep transfer of sovereignty to solve the problems raised by direct State involvement in the Economy. And the entry into force in 1999 of a procedural regulation regarding State Aids has been an important and recent achievement. This regulation codifies the procedural rules and makes them transparent, thereby increasing legal certainty. The Commission can really force Member States to require interim recovery of illegally granted aid. It also sets time limits for State Aid decisions. There are other improvements being prepared such as Block exemption Regulations, a Public register and a Scoreboard that will trace the performance of each Member State in the field of State Aids, thus adding peer pressure to the legal enforcement instruments.

Source: EU Commission.

CHAPTER VIII

Possible aspects of consumer protection

In a number of countries, consumer protection legislation is separate from restrictive business practices legislation.

COMMENTARIES ON CHAPTER VIII AND ALTERNATIVE APPROACHES IN EXISTING LEGISLATIONS

Possible aspects of consumer protection

155. In a number of countries, consumer protection legislation is separate from restrictive business practices legislation.

156. In some countries, however, such as Australia, Hungary, Poland and France, the competition law contains a chapter devoted to consumer protection. Undoubtedly, competition issues are closely related to protection of consumers' economic interests. This is also the case, for example, in Lithuania and Venezuela, where their competition laws contain regulations on "unfair trade practices". In Canada, the Competition Act contains provisions relating to misleading advertising and deceptive marketing practices that are designed to provide consumers with basic uniform and accurate information on certain consumer products and to avoid deceptive and false representations. The text of UNCTAD Model

Law or Laws (1984 version), in TD/B/RBP/15/Rev.1, listed some elements that could be considered by States for inclusion in their restrictive business practices legislation. However, the present trend in countries adopting such legislation seems to be the adoption of two separate laws, one on RBPs or competition, and the others on consumer protection. Nevertheless, because of the links between the two bodies of law, the administration of these laws is often the responsibility of the same authority. This is the case, for example, in Algeria, Australia, Colombia, Costa Rica, Finland, France, New Zealand, Panama, Peru, Poland, the Russian Federation, Sri Lanka, the United Kingdom, the United States and Italy, at least to a certain extent. In Canada, jurisdiction over consumer protection issues and competition issues is divided between the federal government, provincial and territorial governments. The federal government is responsible for the regulation of interprovincial trade and the establishment of national standards to ensure a fair, efficient and competitive marketplace. The provincial and territorial governments assume responsibility for contractual matters relating to the sale and purchase of goods and services. In Estonia, consumer protection legislation and Consumer Protection Authority is separate from competition legislation and Competition Board. However, Estonian Competition Act contains provisions on unfair trade practices but the existence or absence of unfair competition will be ascertained in a court dispute between parties held pursuant to civil procedure. In Zambia, consumer protection legislation is covered under section 12 of the

Competition Law. However, does not deal with matters relating to consumer welfare such as the Public Health, the Standards, the Sales, and Hire Purchase. Therefore, in administering consumer protection, the Competition Commission works closely with other bodies such as local authorities, the Bureau of Standards and the public health service.

157. It is also important to take into account the United Nations General Assembly resolution on Consumer Protection[159] in which comprehensive guidelines on this issue were adopted in 1985. This set includes, *inter alia*, measures devoted to the promotion and protection of consumers' economic interests, along with standards for the safety and quality of consumer goods and services; distribution facilities for essential consumer goods and services; measures enabling consumers to obtain redress; education and information programmes, etc. In this context the United Nations Guidelines on Consumer Protection refers explicitly to the Set of Principles and Rules for the Control of Restrictive Business Practices and recommends Governments to develop, strengthen or maintain measures relating to the control of restrictive and other abusive business practices which may be harmful to consumers, including means for the enforcement of such measures[160].

CHAPTER IX

The Administering Authority and its organization

1. The establishment of the Administering Authority and its title.

2. Composition of the Authority, including its chairmanship and number of members, and the manner in which they are appointed, including the authority responsible for their appointment.

3. Qualifications of persons appointed.

4. The tenure of office of the chairman and members of the Authority, for a stated period, with or without the possibility of reappointment, and the manner of filling vacancies.

5. Removal of members of the Authority.

6. Possible immunity of members against prosecution or any claim relating to the performance of their duties or discharge of their functions.

7. The appointment of necessary staff.

COMMENTARIES ON CHAPTER IX AND ALTERNATIVE APPROACHES IN EXISTING LEGISLATIONS

The Administering Authority and its organization

1. The establishment of the Administering Authority and its title.

158. Section E.1 of the Set of Principles and Rules requires States to adopt, improve and effectively enforce appropriate legislation and to implement judicial and administrative procedures in this area. Recent enactments of legislation and legislative amendments in different countries show trends towards the creation of new bodies for the control of restrictive business practices, or changes in the existing authorities in order to confer additional powers on them and make them more efficient in their functioning.

159. In some cases, there has been a merging of different bodies into one empowered with all functions in the area of restrictive business practices, consumer protection or corporate law. This is the case, for example, in Pakistan where the Government decided to establish a corporate authority to administer the Monopolies Ordinance together with other business laws[161]. This applies also to Colombia[162] and Peru[163].

2. Composition of the Authority, including its chairmanship and number of members, and the manner in which they are appointed, including the authority responsible for their appointment.

160. It is not possible to indicate which should be the appropriate authority. It is also not possible to lay down how the Authority should be integrated into the administrative or judicial machinery of a given country. This is a matter for each country to decide. The present Model Law has been formulated on the assumption that probably the most efficient type of administrative authority is one which is a quasi autonomous or independent body of the Government, with strong judicial and administrative powers for conducting investigations, applying sanctions, etc., while at the same time providing for the possibility of recourse to a higher judicial body. Note that the trend in most of the competition authorities

created in the recent past (usually in developing countries and countries in transition) is to award them as much administrative independence as possible. This feature is very important because it protects the Authority from political influence.

161. The number of members of the Authority differs from country to country. In some legislation the number is not fixed and may vary within a minimum and maximum number, such as in Switzerland and India. Other countries state in their legislation the exact number of members, for example Algeria, Argentina, Brazil, Bulgaria, Côte d'Ivoire, Costa Rica, Hungary, Malta, Mexico, Panama, Peru, Portugal, the Republic of Korea and the Russian Federation. Other countries, such as Australia, have left to the appropriate authority the choice of the number of members. In many countries, the law leaves to the highest authority the appointment of the Chairman and the members of the Commission. In other countries, a high governmental official is designated to occupy the post by the law. In Argentina, the President of the Commission is an Under Secretary of Commerce, and the members are appointed by the Minister of Economics[164]. In some countries, such as India, Malta and Pakistan, it is obligatory to publish the appointments in the official gazettes for public knowledge. Certain legislation establishes the internal structure and the functioning of the Authority and establish rules for its operation, while others leave such details to the Authority itself[165]. In Chile, both the Resolutive Commission and the Preventive Commissions consist of five members. (See articles 7, 10 and 16 of Decree Law No. 211.)

162. A tendency observed in some countries is the partial or total change regarding the origin of the members of the national authorities in relation to restrictive business practices. This is the case in Chile where under previous legislation members of the Resolutive Commission were basically officers from the public administration, while at present such posts include representatives from the University[166]. This is, in effect, a way of striking a balance between juridical and economic matters. It may also be pointed out that the membership of the Preventive Commissions includes a spokesman of the residents' associations of the capital city of the given region, representing the views of consumers.

163. In Zambia, section 4 of the Act establishes the Zambia Competition Commission (ZCC) which shall be a Statutory body corporate with perpetual succession and a common seal, capable of suing and being sued.

ZCC is supervised by the Board of Commissioners appointed under Article 1 of the schedule. The Board of Commissioners consists of 13 persons drawn from government, trade, professional and consumer associations. The Board members are appointed for a fixed term of three years but renewable for re-appointment. The members of the board are appointed by their respective associations they represent. The Minister does not appoint any member but only formalizes the appointments. The Board, including the Chairman, is part-time.

In Zambia, there are specific minimum qualifications except that a member must be nominated by the relevant trade or professional association specified in the Act. The Chairman and members of the Commission in Zambia are appointed for a period of 3 years, renewable for a further 3 years (thus 6 years in total).   Article 10 of the schedule to the Act provides that no action or other proceeding shall lie against any member, member of staff, servant, agent or representative of the Commission for or in respect of any act done or omitted to be done in good faith in the exercise or purported exercise of his functions under the Act. The Board of Commissioners appoints the Executive Director (CEO) and other staff as it considers necessary for the performance of its functions under the Act[167].

3.   Qualifications of persons appointed.

164. Several laws establish the qualifications that any person should have in order to become a member of the Authority. For example, in Peru members of the Multi sectorial Free Competition Commission must have a professional degree and at least 10 years of experience in its respective field of knowledge. In Brazil, members of the Administrative Economic Protection Council are chosen among citizens reputed for their legal and economic knowledge and unblemished reputation[168]. In Chile, the National Economic Prosecutor must be a lawyer and have 10 years' professional experience or three years' seniority in service. The Deputy Prosecutor, for his part, must also hold the title of lawyer and have a minimum of 5 years' professional experience or specialization in areas related to the functions of the Prosecutor's Office.

165. In a number of countries the legislation states that the persons in question should not have interests which would conflict with the functions to be performed. In India, for example, a person should not have any financial

or other interest likely to affect prejudicially his functions. In Germany, members must not be owners, chairmen or members of the board of management or the supervisory board of any enterprise, cartel, trade industry association, or professional association. In Hungary, the President, vice presidents, Competition Council members and other civil servant staff members of the competition authority may not pursue activities for profit other than those dedicated to scientific, educational, artistic, authorial and inventive pursuits, as well as activities arising out of legal relationships aimed at linguistic and editorial revision, and may not serve as senior officials of a business organization, or members of a supervisory board or board of directors[169]. Similar provisions are included in the Italian and Mexican legislation. In Chile, it is stipulated that the persons who serve in the National Economic Prosecutor's Office cannot serve as dependent workers or exercise other related activities as natural or legal persons who might be subject to action by the National Economic Prosecutor's Office. Furthermore, all members of the Commissions, whatever the capacity in which they act, as well as the consultants and advisers receiving honoraria from the National Economic Prosecutor's Office, are considered as public employees for all legal purposes[170].

4. The tenure of office of the chairman and members of the Authority, for a stated period, with or without the possibility of reappointment, and the manner of filling vacancies.

166. The tenure in office of the members of the Administering Authority varies from country to country. At present, members are appointed in Italy for 7 years, in Hungary for 6 years, in Algeria and Panama for 5 years, in Argentina for 4 years and Mexico for 10 years, and in Bulgaria, and Pakistan for 5 years. In Canada, the Commissioner of Competition is head of the Competition Bureau and is appointed for a 5 year term. In Lithuania, the law refers to a tenure of 6 years. In Brazil it is for 2 years, and in other countries, such as Peru and Switzerland, it is for an indefinite period. In many countries, such as Thailand, the Republic of Korea, Argentina, India, Canada and Australia, members have the possibility of being reappointed, but in the case of Brazil this is possible only once. In the UK, the period of tenure of office of members of the Administering Authority varies as between the Competition Commission and the DGFT and it is not yet clear what the position will be with regard to new OFT Board Members who will be taking office in the course of 2003[171]. In Australia

members of the Commission are appointed for a period of up to 5 years and can be reappointed. In Chile, the tenure of office of members of the Commissions is two years. In the event of an impediment, they will be replaced by an alternate member.

5. Removal of members of the Authority.

167. Legislation in several countries provides an appropriate authority with powers to remove from office a member of the Administering Authority that has engaged in certain actions or has become unfit for the post. For example, becoming physically incapable is a reason for removal in Hungary, Thailand, the Republic of Korea and India; becoming bankrupt, in Thailand, India and Australia; in Mexico[172], they can only be removed "for a duly substantiated serious" failing in the obligations that one acquires as a member of the Administering Authority, in Argentina and Australia; being absent from duty, in Australia. Another cause for removal is being sentenced to disciplinary punishment or dismissal, for example in Hungary[173] or imprisonment in Thailand. In the People's Republic of China where a staff member of the State organ monitoring and investigating practices of unfair competition acts irregularly out of personal considerations and intentionally screens an operator from prosecution, fully knowing that he had contravened the provisions of China's law, constituting a crime, the said staff member shall be prosecuted for his criminal liability according to law[174]. The procedure for removal varies from country to country. In Panama, the agency might be appointed by the Executive, and approved by the Legislature, from lists of candidates to be presented by various representative bodies of civil society (universities, professional associations of economists and lawyers, entrepreneurial unions, etc.), for a period concurrent with that of the Executive. The dismissal or removal of appointees might be effected, subject to the prior favourable opinion of the Judiciary, due to:

i) Permanent incapacity to carry out their duties

ii) Declaration of bankruptcy or manifest insolvency

iii) Conviction for offences against patrimony, public trust or public administration

iv) Repeated negligence in the performance of their functions[175]

6. Possible immunity of members against prosecution or any claim relating to the performance of their duties or discharge of their functions.

168.   In order to protect the members and officers of the Administering Authority from prosecution and claims, full immunity may be given to them when carrying out their functions. In Pakistan, for example, the Authority or any of its officials or servants have immunity against any suit, prosecution or other legal proceeding for anything done in good faith or intended to be done under the Monopolies Law.

7. The appointment of necessary staff.

169.   There are variations for the appointment of staff of the Administering Authority. In some countries, as in Pakistan and Sri Lanka, the Administering Authority appoints its own staff. In others, the Government has this power.

CHAPTER X

Functions and powers of the Administering Authority

I.   *The functions and powers of the Administering Authority could include (illustrative):*

(a) Making inquiries and investigations, including as a result of receipt of complaints;

(b) Taking the necessary decisions, including the imposition of sanctions, or recommending same to a responsible minister;

(c) Undertaking studies, publishing reports and providing information to the public;

(d) Issuing forms and maintaining a register, or registers, for notifications;

(e) Making and issuing regulations;

(f) Assisting in the preparation, amending or review of legislation on restrictive business practices, or on related areas of regulation and competition policy;

(g) Promoting exchange of information with other States.

II.   *Confidentiality*

1. According information obtained from enterprises containing legitimate business secrets reasonable safeguards to protect its confidentiality.

2. Protecting the identity of persons who provide information to competition authorities and who need confidentiality to protect themselves against economic retaliation.

3. Protecting the deliberations of government in regard to current or still uncompleted matters.

COMMENTARIES ON CHAPTER X AND ALTERNATIVE APPROACHES IN EXISTING LEGISLATIONS

Functions and powers of the Administering Authority

I.   *The functions and powers of the Administering Authority could include (illustrative):*

170.   Most legislation dealing with restrictive business practices establishes a list of the functions and powers that the Authority possesses for carrying out its tasks, and which provide a general framework for its operations. An illustrative list of functions of the Authority is contained in article 8. It is important to mention that all these functions are related to the activities that the Competition Authority or competition enforcement agency might develop, as well as the means usually at its disposal for carrying out its tasks. A common feature to be highlighted is that the Authority's functions must be based on the principle of due process of law as well as transparency.

(a) Making inquiries and investigations, including as a result of receipt of complaints;

171.   The Authority may act on its own initiative, or following certain indications that the restrictive practice exists for example, as a result of a complaint made by any person or enterprise. Box 15 gives examples of information to be supplied to the Competition Authority in a complaint. Information gathered by other government departments, such as the internal revenue, foreign trade, customs or foreign exchange control authorities, if applicable, may also provide a necessary source of information. The Principles and Rules specify that States

---

Box 15

Investigation procedures

(i)   Information to be supplied to the Competition Authority in a complaint

·   Details about the complainant and about the firm(s) complained of;

·   Details about the substance of the complaint;

·   Evidence as to why the complainant has a legitimate interest;

·   Details of whether a similar complaint has been made to any other authorities (e.g. sectoral ministries or agencies) or is the subject of proceedings in a court;

·   Details of any products or services involved and a description of the relevant market;

·   A statement of what remedies are sought from the Competition Authority (including interim remedies).

(ii)   Examples of documents which the Competition Authority may inspect

·   Financial records;

·   Sales records;

·   Production records;

·   Travel records;

·   Diaries;

·   Minutes or notes of meetings held either internally, or with third parties;

·   Records and copies of correspondence (internal and external), personal memoranda, including telephone numbers and fax numbers used during particular periods, records of electronic mail;

·   Photographic materials.

Sources: European Commission and OECD.

---

should institute or improve procedures for obtaining information from enterprises necessary for their effective control of restrictive business practices. The Authority should also be empowered to order persons or enterprises to provide information and to call for and receive testimony. In the event that this information is not supplied, the obtaining of a search warrant or a court order may be envisaged, where applicable, in order to require that information be furnished and/or to permit entry into premises where information is believed to be located. Box 15 provides examples of documents which the Competition Authority may inspect. Finally, it is indispensable to mention that in the process of investigation, the general principles and rules of due process of law, which in many countries is a constitutional mandate, must be duly observed.

172.   In many countries, including Argentina, Australia, Germany, Italy, Hungary, Norway, Pakistan, Peru and the Russian Federation, as well as in the European Community, the Administering Authority has the power to order enterprises to supply information and to authorize a staff member to enter premises in search of relevant information. However, entry into premises may be subject to certain conditions. For example, in Argentina a court order is required for entry into private dwellings, while in Germany searches, while normally requiring a court order, can be conducted without one if there is a "danger in delay".

(b) Taking the necessary decisions, including the imposition of sanctions, or recommending same to a responsible minister;

173.   The Administering Authority would need, as a result of inquiries and investigations undertaken, to take certain decisions as, for example, to initiate proceedings or call for the discontinuation of certain practices, or to deny or grant authorization of matters notified, or to impose sanctions, as the case may be.

(c) Undertaking studies, publishing reports and providing information to the public;

174.   The Authority could undertake studies and obtain expert assistance for its own studies, or commission studies from outside. In Brazil, for example, the law establishes that the Economic Law Office of the Ministry of Justice shall carry out studies and research with a view to improving antitrust policies. Some legislation explicitly requests the authorities to engage in particular studies. For example, in Thailand the Office on Price Fixing and Anti Monopoly has the power and the duty to study, analyse and conduct research concerning goods, prices and business operations; in Argentina, the Commission can prepare studies related to markets, including research into how their conduct affects the interests of consumers, and in Portugal the Council for Competition may request the Directorate General for Competition and Prices to undertake appropriate studies in order to formulate opinions to be submitted to the Minister responsible for trade[176]. The Authority could inform the public of its activities regularly. Periodic reports are useful for this purpose and most of the countries that have restrictive business practices legislation issue at least an annual report.

(d) Issuing forms and maintaining a register, or registers, for notifications;

175.   The laws of most countries having notification procedures include provision for some system of registration which must be characterized by transparency. This is the case, for example, of Spain, with the Registry for Safeguarding Competition, and France at the level of the Directorate General for Competition, Consumers Affairs and Frauds Repression (DGCCRF)[177]. Some countries maintain a public register in which certain, but not all, of the information provided through notification is recorded. The usefulness of a public register lies in the belief that publicity can operate to some extent as a

deterrent to enterprises engaging in restrictive business practices, as well as provide an opportunity for persons affected by such practices to be informed of them. Such persons can also make specific complaints and advise of any inaccuracies in the information notified. However, not all the information notified can be registered, and one of the reasons for this is that certain information will relate to so called "business secrets", and disclosure could affect the operations of the enterprise in question. Sensitive business information in the hands of the competition authorities cannot be overstated because a breach of such confidentiality will strongly discourage the business community from quick compliance with reasonable requests for information.

(e) Making and issuing regulations;

176.   The Authority should also have powers to issue implementing regulations to assist it in accomplishing its tasks.

(f) Assisting in the preparation, amending or review of legislation on restrictive business practices, or on related areas of regulation and competition policy;

177.   Owing to the high level of specialization and the unique experience of the Administering Authority in the field of competition, a growing number of new laws or amendments give the Authority the additional responsibility for advising on the draft bills which may affect competition, as well as for studying and submitting to the Government the appropriate proposals for the amendment of legislation on competition. This is the case, for example, in Bulgaria at the level of the Commission for the Protection of Competition[178], Portugal with its Council for Competition, which can formulate opinions, give advice and provide guidance in competition policy matters[179], Spain, at the level of the Court for the Protection of Competition[180].

(g) Promoting exchange of information with other States.

178.   The Principles and Rules require States to establish appropriate mechanisms at the regional and subregional levels to promote exchange of information on restrictive business practices. It would be convenient to provide the Authority with the power to promote such exchange by clearly establishing it as one of its functions. For example, under the legislation of Belgium it is possible to communicate the necessary documents and information

to the appropriate foreign authorities for competition matters, under agreements regarding reciprocity in relation to mutual assistance concerning competitive practices[181]. Information exchange and consultations are also provided for in bilateral agreements between the United States, Australia, Brazil, Canada, Germany, Israel, Japan, Mexico and the Commission of the European Communities, as well as between France and Germany and also a multilateral agreement between Denmark, Iceland and Norway. In addition, it is provided for in Section F (4) of the Set.

II. *Confidentiality*

1. According information obtained from enterprises containing legitimate business secrets reasonable safeguards to protect its confidentiality.

2. Protecting the identity of persons who provide information to competition authorities and who need confidentiality to protect themselves against economic retaliation.

3. Protecting the deliberations of government in regard to current or still uncompleted matters.

179. In accordance with paragraph 5 of section E of the Set of Principles and Rules, legitimate business secrets should be accorded the normally applicable safeguards, in particular to protect their confidentiality. The confidential information submitted to the Administering Authority or obtained by it can also be protected, in general, by the national legislation regarding secrecy. Nevertheless, in some countries such as Mexico[182], Portugal[183], and Switzerland[184] their legislation contains special provisions on the secrecy of the evidence obtained during the proceedings. According to the Estonian Competition Act 63 (1), the Competition Board does not have the right to disclose the business secrets, including information subject to banking secrecy, of an undertaking which have become known to the Competition Board in the course of performance of its official duties to other persons or to publish them without the consent of the undertaking. Taiwan, Province of China, signed a trilateral cooperation arrangement with the Commerce Commission of New Zealand and ACCC of Australia in July 2002 and has a bilateral cooperation arrangement with the two agencies respectively, including provisions dealing with confidentiality.

CHAPTER XI

Sanctions and relief

I. *The imposition of sanctions, as appropriate, for:*

   (i) Violations of the law;

   (ii) Failure to comply with decisions or orders of the Administering Authority, or of the appropriate judicial authority;

   (iii) Failure to supply information or documents required within the time limits specified;

   (iv) Furnishing any information, or making any statement, which the enterprise knows, or has any reason to believe, to be false or misleading in any material sense.

II. *Sanctions could include:*

   (i) Fines (in proportion to the secrecy, gravity and clear cut illegality of offences or in relation to the illicit gain achieved by the challenged activity);

   (ii) Imprisonment (in cases of major violations involving flagrant and intentional breach of the law, or of an enforcement decree, by a natural person);

   (iii) Interim orders or injunctions;

   (iv) Permanent or long term orders to cease and desist or to remedy a violation by positive conduct, public disclosure or apology, etc.;

   (v) Divestiture (in regard to completed mergers or acquisitions), or rescission (in regard to certain mergers, acquisitions or restrictive contracts);

   (vi) Restitution to injured consumers;

   (vii)Treatment of the administrative or judicial finding or illegality as prima facie evidence of liability in all damage actions by injured persons.

COMMENTARIES ON CHAPTER XI AND ALTERNATIVE APPROACHES IN EXISTING LEGISLATIONS

Sanctions and relief

I. *The imposition of sanctions, as appropriate, for:*

(i) Violations of the law;

(ii) Failure to comply with decisions or orders of the Administering Authority, or of the appropriate judicial authority;

(iii) Failure to supply information or documents required within the time limits specified;

(iv) Furnishing any information, or making any statement, which the enterprise knows, or has any reason to believe, to be false or misleading in any material sense.

180. Subparagraph II of article 10 lists a number of possible sanctions for breaches enumerated in subparagraph I.

II. *Sanctions could include:*

(i) Fines (in proportion to the secrecy, gravity and clear cut illegality of offences or in relation to the illicit gain achieved by the challenged activity);

181. The power to impose fines on enterprises and individuals may be vested either in the Administering Authority, or in the judicial authority, or it may be divided between the two. In the latter case, for example, the Authority's power to impose fines might be limited to such conduct as refusals to supply information, the giving of false information and failure to modify agreements. In Norway, the NCA may issue a writ giving an option of relinquishment of gain according to section 6-5 of the law, but this is not a traditional competition fine.

In Pakistan, Panama, Peru, the Russian Federation and Switzerland, and in the EC, the administering bodies have powers to impose fines. In Australia and the United States of America, the power to impose fines is vested in the courts. The maximum amount of fines varies of course from country to country.

182. Fines may also vary according to the type of infringement (in India and Portugal), or according to whether the infringement was committed wilfully or negligently (Germany and the EC), or they may be expressed in terms of a specific figure and/or in terms of the minimum or reference salary (Brazil, Mexico, Peru, Russian Federation), and/or they may be calculated in relation to the profits made as a result of the infringement (China, Germany, Hungary). Moreover, in certain countries, such as Germany, an offence can be punished by a fine of up to three times the additional receipt obtained as a result of the infringement. Treble damages are also important in cases of price fixing in the United States. In Peru, in case of recurrence the fine could be doubled[185].

183. It would seem logical that the fines be indexed to inflation, and that account be taken of both the gravity of the offences and the ability to pay by enterprises, so that the smaller enterprises would not be penalized in the same manner as large ones, for which fines having a low ceiling would constitute small disincentive for engaging in restrictive practices.

184. Recent enforcement attitudes towards arrangements have been to seek deterrence by means of very substantial fines for companies. In the European Community, fines imposed by the Commission can reach up to 10 per cent of the annual turnover (of all products) of the offending enterprises. Hence, in 1991, Tetra Pak was found to infringe article 86 of the Treaty of Rome (abuse of a dominant position) and, consequently, a fine of 75 million ECUs was imposed. Such a firm attitude towards infringement of EC competition law was confirmed in the case of three cartels (on steel bars, carton and cement), which were condemned in 1994 to pay fines of ECU 104, 132.15 and 248 million respectively[186]. In the United States, legislation was enacted in 1990 raising the maximum corporate fine for an antitrust violation from US$ 1 million to US$ 10 million[187]. In Japan, legislation has been introduced to allow fines of up to 6 per cent of the total commerce affected over a three year period. Under this legislation, a fine of US$ 80 million was imposed by the Japanese Fair Trade Commission on a cement cartel in 1991. In Ukraine, fines can be up to 10% of income of the entity. In the Zambian legislation, Penalties include a fine not exceeding 10 million Kwacha (US$2,500) or a prison term not exceeding 5 years or to both. Such penalties cannot be imposed by the Zambia Competition Commission but a court of law. However, most cases are resolved through a consultative and arbitration approach, by way of restitution to affected customers, divestiture, discontinuation of anti competitive

arrangements etc. In Chile, the fines may be up to approximately US$ 400,000, the amount being determined by the Tribunal duly taking into consideration the offender's turnover and economic capacity and the gravity of the infraction. In Panama, the sanctions (fines) could also be proportional to the volume of transactions and business of the enterprises that have violated the law (calculated as a percentage of their income from sales).

   (ii) Imprisonment (in cases of major violations involving flagrant and intentional breach of the law, or of an enforcement decree, by a natural person);

185. The power to impose imprisonment would normally be vested in the judicial authority. In certain countries, such as Japan and Norway, the power to impose terms of imprisonment is reserved for the judicial authorities on the application of the Administering Authority. Terms of imprisonment may be up to one, two, three or more years, depending upon the nature of the offence.

186. In countries such as Argentina and Canada, where the judicial authorities are responsible for decisions under the restrictive business practices legislation, the courts have the power to impose prison sentences of up to six years (Argentina) and up to five years (Canada). In the United States, criminal antitrust offences are limited to clearly defined "per se" unlawful conduct and defendant's conduct which is manifestly anti competitive: price fixing, bid rigging, and market allocation. Only the Sherman Act provides criminal penalties (violations for Sections 1 and 2) and infractions may be prosecuted as a felony punishable by a corporate fine and three years' imprisonment for individuals. In the United States Antitrust Division prosecution of Sherman Act, criminal penalties are governed by general federal criminal statutes, the Federal Rules of Criminal Procedure[188] and the U.S. Sentencing Guidelines. The United Kingdom recently introduced, under the Enterprise Act 2003, criminal sanctions for individuals who participate in certain clearly defined anti-competitive offences. In Estonia all competition offences are criminal in nature, and the Competition Board has the right to conduct pre-trial investigations. In cases of cooperation of particular enterprises in the identification and eventual sanctioning of anti-competitive conduct, in which the given enterprises participated, these enterprises could be granted an exemption from the sanctions so as to encourage the instability of the cartels.

   (iii) Interim orders or injunctions;

187. In Hungary, the Competition Council may, by an interim measure, prohibit in its decision the continuation of the illegal conduct or order the elimination of the illegal state of affairs, if prompt action is required for the protection of the legal or economic interests of the interested persons or because the formation, development or continuation of economic competition is threatened. The Competition Council may also require a bond as a condition[189].

   (iv) Permanent or long term orders to cease and desist or to remedy a violation by positive conduct, public disclosure or apology, etc.;

188. An example is provided by Korean FTC when the United States limited the import of colour television sets from the Republic of Korea. Samsung, Gold Star and Daewoo cut prices locally to increase sales, but then agreed with each other to cease cutting prices. The Fair Trade Office ordered an end to the price fixing and required the companies to apologize in a local newspaper[190].

189. Within this framework, and as an additional measure, the possibility may be considered of publishing cease and desist orders as well as the final sentence imposing whatever sanction the administrative or judicial authority have considered adequate, as is the case in France[191] and in the European Community. In this way the business community and especially consumers would be in a position to know that a particular enterprise has engaged in unlawful behaviour.

   (v) Divestiture (in regard to completed mergers or acquisitions), or rescission (in regard to certain mergers, acquisitions or restrictive contracts);

190. This clause is applied in Mexico, where the Commission can order "partial or total deconcentration" of the merger[192]. In the United States, divestiture is a remedy in cases of unlawful mergers and acquisitions[193]. It is also to be noted that divestment powers could be extended to include dominant positions[194].

   (vi) Restitution to injured consumers;

   (vii) Treatment of the administrative or judicial finding or illegality as prima facie evidence of liability in all damage actions by injured persons.

CHAPTER XII

Appeals

1. Request for review by the Administering Authority of its decisions in the light of changed circumstances.

2. Affording the possibility for any enterprise or individual to appeal within (...) days to the (appropriate judicial authority) against the whole or any part of the decision of the Administering Authority, (or) on any substantive point of law.

COMMENTARIES ON CHAPTER XII AND ALTERNATIVE APPROACHES IN EXISTING LEGISLATIONS

Appeals

1. Request for review by the Administering Authority of its decisions in light of changed circumstances.

2. Affording the possibility for any enterprise or individual to appeal within (...) days to the (appropriate judicial authority) against the whole or any part of the decision of the Administering Authority, (or) on any substantive point of law.

191. Concerning the review of the administering authorities' decisions, in many instances, the circumstances prevailing at the time of decision making may change. It is recalled that the Administering Authority can, for example, periodically or because of a change of circumstances review authorizations granted and possibly extend, suspend or subject the extension to the *fulfilment* of conditions and obligations. Therefore, enterprises should be equally given the possibility of requesting review of decisions, when circumstances prompting the decisions have changed or have ceased to exist.

192. The right of a person to appeal against the decision of the Administrative Authority is specifically provided for in the law of most countries (for example, Lithuania[195] and the Russian Federation[196]) or, without specific mention, may exist automatically under the civil, criminal or administrative procedural codes (for example, Colombia[197] and Portugal[198]). Competition laws of many countries appropriately provide various grounds for appellate review, including review (under various standards) on findings of fact and conclusions of law made in the initial decision. In other countries, appeals are possible in cases specifically mentioned in the competition law, as is the case, for example, with decisions of the Swedish Competition Authority[199].

193. Appeals may involve a rehearing of the case or be limited, as in Brazil, India and Pakistan, to a point of law. In Italy, appeals against administrative measures adopted by the Italian Competition Authority fall within the exclusive jurisdiction of the Regional Administrative Tribunal of Latium (which is the part of judiciary competent for administrative matters) with the exceptions of the annulment proceedings and claims for damages, and petitions for emergency measures that must be filed before the competent Court of Appeal. Appeals may be made to administrative courts, as in Gabon, Lithuania, Colombia, Venezuela and Zambia or to judicial courts, as in Algeria, Côte d'Ivoire, Panama, Spain, Switzerland and Ukraine, or to both, as in the Russian Federation, where an appeal may be lodged in an ordinary court or a court of arbitration[200]. In this connection, a special administrative court may be created, as for example, in Australia[201], Denmark[202], Kenya[203], Peru[204], and Spain[205]. In India and Pakistan appeals go directly to the Supreme Court and the High Court, respectively. This is also true for Peru, where appeals go directly to the Supreme Court of Justice. In Germany, appeals may go through the courts. Alternatively, in the case of a merger which has been blocked by the Administrative Authority, the parties can request exceptional approval from the Minister of Economic Affairs. In Austria appeals go to the Superior Cartel Court at the Supreme Court of Justice.

194. The European Community has created a specialized Court of First Instance to hear antitrust appeals, since such cases had begun to be a burden on the European Court of Justice because of the extensive factual records involved.

CHAPTER XIII

Actions for damages

To afford a person, or the State on behalf of the person who, or an enterprise which, suffers loss or damages by an act or omission of any enterprise or individual in contravention of the provisions of the law, to be entitled to recover the amount of the loss or damage (including costs and interest) by legal action before the appropriate judicial authorities.

COMMENTARIES ON CHAPTER XIII AND DIFFERENT APPROACHES IN EXISTING LEGISLATIONS

Actions for damages

To afford a person, or the State on behalf of the person who, or an enterprise which, suffers loss or damages by an act or omission of any enterprise or individual in contravention of the provisions of the law, to be entitled to recover the amount of the loss or damage (including costs and interest) by legal action before the appropriate judicial authorities.

195. The proposed provision would give the right to an individual or to the State on behalf of an individual, or to an enterprise to bring a suit in respect of breaches of law, in order to recover damages suffered, including costs and interests accrued. Such civil action would normally be conducted through the appropriate judicial authorities, as is the case of the European Community, unless States specifically empower the Administering Authority in this regard. Provision for State *parens patriae* suit is found in a number of laws of developed countries[206]. Under such "class actions", users or consumers of a specific service or good who have suffered damage from *anti competitive* behaviour, and whose individual claim would be too insignificant, have the right to institute action against enterprises. This is considered in the laws of Canada, France and the United States.

196. In certain countries competitors or injured persons are generally authorized to sue for violations against the economic order, including price fixing, predatory pricing and tying agreements. This is the case under the laws of Colombia, Estonia, Mexico[207], Peru[208], South Africa, Taiwan, Province of China, Venezuela[209] and Zambia.

Notes

[1]   Cf. for example, Colombia, Finland, Hungary, India, Switzerland.

[2]   Cf. Chile, Japan, Poland.

[3]   Countries referring to the concept of "competition" in their Law include i.e Algeria, Argentina, Brazil, Canada, Côte d'Ivoire, Denmark, European Union, France, Germany, Greece, India, Italy, Lithuania, Mexico, Morocco, the Netherlands, Norway, Panama, Portugal, Spain, Sweden, Tunisia, United Kingdom. See also the list of some names of competition laws of the world in annex 1.

[4]   Ordinance No. 95 06 of 23 Chabane 1415 of 25 January 1995 concerning Competition. Article 1.

[5]   Competition Act of 1985. Section 1.1. (Canada)

[6]   Law No. 014/98 of 23 July 1998 establishing the competition regime in the Gabonese Republic, Article 2.2.

[7]   Competition Act of 2002. Section 1.

[8]   Act No. LVII of 1996 on the Prohibition of Unfair and Restrictive Market Practices. Introduction.

[9]   Law of Mongolia on Prohibiting Unfair Competition. Article 1.

[10]   Act 65 of 11 June 1993 relating to Competition in Commercial Activity. Section 1.1 (The purpose of the Act). This law is referred to as the Competition Act and entered into force on 1 January 1994. (Norway)

[11]   Law No. 29 of 1 February 1996 on Rules for Protecting Competition and other Measures. Article 1. (Panama)

[12]   Legislative Decree No. 701 Against Monopolistic, Control and Restrictive Practices Affecting Free Competition. Article 2. (Peru)

[13]   Law of 30 May 1995 on Competition and the Limitation of Monopolistic Activity in Commodity Markets. Article 1. (Russian Federation)

[14]   Law 16 / 1989 on the Protection of Competition. (Spain)

[15]   Competition Act (1993:20) of 14 January 1993. Section 1. (Sweden)

[16]   Federal Law on Cartels and other Restrictions on Competition of 6 October 1995 (Lcart. RS 251, FF 1995 I 472. First Article). (Switzerland)

[17]   Northern Pacific Railway Co. v. United States, 356 U.S. 1, 4, 78 S.CT. 514, 517, 2 L. Ed.2d 545, 549 (1958).

[18]   Fair Trade Law 1992. (Taiwan Province of China)

[19]   Law to Promote and Protect the Exercise of Free Competition. Article 1. (Venezuela)

[20]   Competition and Fair Trading Act 1994.

[21]   Decision 285 of the Commission of the Cartagena Agreement. Article 1.

[22]   Treaty establishing the European Economic Community (Treaty of Rome). Rome, 25 March 1957. In particular articles 2 and 3 (f).

[23]   Trade Practices Act, 1974. As amended. Section 45. (Australia)

24   Article 10 of the Federal Law on Economic Competition. (Mexico)

25   The United Kingdom Competition Act Chapter 1. 1998.

26   Treaty establishing the European Economic Community (Treaty of Rome). Rome, 25 March 1957.

27   See: TD/B/RBP/15/Rev.1, paras. 24 to 26.

28   The United Kingdom Competition Act Chapter 1. 1995 and Treaty establishing the European Economic
        Community (Treaty of Rome). Rome, 25 March 1957.

29   It should be noted that a competition authority, particularly if it is an independent administrative body, will
        not have the political mandate to determine how certain restrictions would affect the "national interest", or
        influence a country's "overall economic development". Because of this, authorizations should be based, in
        principle, on competition concerns. As an alternative, Governments might consider the possibility that their
        national authorities could assist the Government in the preparation, amending or reviewing of legislation that
        might affect competition, such as mentioned in article 8 (1) (f) of the Model Law, and give its advisory
        opinion on any proposed measure that might have an impact on competition.

30   United States Department of Justice/Federal Trade Commission Horizontal Merger Guidelines, 2 April
        1992.

31   National Soc. of Professional Engineers v. United States, 435 U.S. 679, 692 (1978).

32   Standard Oil Co. of California and Standard Stations Inc. v. United States. United States Supreme Court,
        1949. 337 U.S. 293,299 S.Ct 1051, 93 L.Ed. 1371.

33   The Competition Act 2002 Section 2(4). (India)

34   Producers might by anti-competitive agreement avoid operating in particular areas and that would not be
        a reason for defining a geographical market narrowly (comment transmitted by the Government of the
        United Kingdom).

35   Information provided by the Government of the United Kingdom.

36   The Anti-Monopoly Law (1973 rev. 1980 rev. 2002). (Chile)

37   See for example as regards Italian Customs agents Case C-35/96 Commission v. Italy (1998 ECRI-
        3851).

38   Law of the 11th January 2001 on the Protection of Economic Competition. (Ukraine)

39   Law of the 6th November 2000on the Protection of Economic Competition. (Armenia)

40   The Competition and Fair Trading Act 1994 and Section 6(i) and Section 3. (Zambia)

41   MERCOSUR/CMC/DEC.No.29/94 on Public Policies that Distort Competitiveness. First Consideration
        Paragraph.

42   Peruvian legislation allows the Administering Authority to investigate and ban those acts by which
        government officials interfere with free competition. In a recent case, the Minister for Economics and
        Finance was summoned to inform about an agreement between the Ministry and various transport associations
        by which urban transportation tariffs were settled at uniform level. The Multi sectorial Free Competition
        Commission considered the agreement as anti competitive and decided that, in future, the Minister should
        refrain from promoting similar agreements (Information submitted by the Peruvian Government).

43   The United Kingdom competition law clearly applies to the commercial activities of local governments,
        which in this respect has no particular status (although many of its activities do not amount to "the supply of
        goods or services" or are not "in the course of business", thereby taking them out of the scope of United

Kingdom competition law). The Crown is immune from action under United Kingdom competition law, but it is notable that not all State activities are Crown activities (for example, the National Health Service). It is also government policy for the Crown to behave as if it were subject to the provisions of competition law in its commercial activities.

44   The restrictive Trade Practices, Monopolies and Trade Control Act 1988 (Kenya) Section 5.

45   Intellectual property law is that area of law which concerns legal rights associated with creative effort or commercial reputation and goodwill. The subject matter of intellectual property is very wide and includes literary and artistic works, films, computer programs, inventions, designs and marks used by traders for their goods and services. The law deters others from copying or taking unfair advantage of the work or reputation of another and provides remedies should it happen (David Bainbridge, *Intellectual Property*, Pitman Publishing, London, 1994, 2 Ed). There are several different forms of rights or areas of law giving rise to rights that together make up intellectual property. Following the results of the Uruguay Round of Multilateral Trade Negotiations (Final Act of the Uruguay Round and the *Marrakech* Agreement Establishing the World Trade Organization), intellectual property refers to the categories that are considered in Sections 1 through 7 Part II of Annex 1C to the Agreement on Trade Related Aspects of Intellectual Property Rights (TRIPs): copyright and related rights, trademarks, geographical indications, industrial designs, patents, layout designs (topographies) of integrated circuits and protection of undisclosed information (trade secrets). It should also consider as intellectual property protection any case of unfair competition (when involving an infringement of an exclusive right) considered under article 10 *bis* of the Paris Convention for the Protection of Industrial Property (1967). It is also important to take note of the Berne Convention for the Protection of Literary and Artistic Works (1971) and the International Convention for the Protection of Performers, Producers of Phonograms and Broadcasting Organizations (1961), also referred to as the "Rome Convention". Commission Regulation (EEC) No. 4087/88 of 30 November 1988 on franchising agreements; Commission Regulation (EEC) No. 556/89 of 30 November 1988 on know how licensing agreements.

46   Royal Decree No. 157/1992 of 21 February 1992, developing Law 16/1989 of 17 July 1989 concerning block exemptions, singular authorizations and a registry for safeguarding competition.BOE 29 February 1992 (RCL 1992, 487). In particular article 1 (f).

47   Section 144 of Copyright, Patents and Designs Act 1988 and Section 51 of Patents Act 1977. Information provided by the Government of the United Kingdom.

48   Antitrust guidelines for licensing of intellectual property, issued by the United States Department of Justice and the Federal Trade Commission, adopted and published on 6 April 1995. It is to be noted that the guidelines state the antitrust enforcement policy to the licensing of intellectual property protected by patent, copyright, and trade secret law, and of know how. They do not cover the antitrust treatment of trademarks. Although the same general antitrust principles that apply to other forms of intellectual property also apply to trademarks, the guidelines deal with technology transfer and innovation related issues that typically arise with respect to patents, copyrights, trade secrets, and know how agreements, rather than with product differentiation issues that typically arise with respect to trademarks.

49   Article 40 (Part II, Section 8) of the Agreement on Trade Related Aspects of Intellectual Property Rights (TRIPs). Annex 1C of the Marrakech Agreement Establishing the World Trade Organization (WTO).

50   The Anti-Monopoly Law, Art.5 (1973 rev. 1980 rev. 2002). (Chile)

51   Centrafarm B.V. v. Sterling Drug, 1974 ECR 1147 (EC); Copperweld Corp. v. Independence Tube Corp., 104 S.CT 2731 (1984).

52   Expanding the rule of Copperweld. Satellite Fin. Planning Corp. v. First National Bank, 633 F. Sup. 386 (D. Del. 1986), but see Sonitrol of Fresno v. AT&T, 1986 1 Trade Cas (CCII) Section 67,080 (32.6 per cent ownership does not establish lack of rivalry).

53   Monopolies and Restrictive Trade Practices (Control and Prevention) Ordinance, 1970, as amended up to 1983. Section 2 (1) (a). (Pakistan)

54   Ordinance No. 95 06 of 25 January 1995 on Competition. Article 6. (Algeria)

55   The Monopolies and Restrictive Trade Practices Act of 1969, as amended up to Act 58 of 1991. Section 2 (a). (South Africa)

56   Law of 24 February 1990 on Counteracting Monopolistic Practices. Article 2 (3) (b). (Poland)

57   Law of 30 May 1995 on Competition and the Limitation of Monopolistic Activity in Commodity Markets. Article 6 (2). Refers to "agreements (coordinating actions) concluded in any form". (Russia)

58   Law to Promote and Protect the Exercise of Free Competition of 1991. Article 5.

59   Concerning the parallel increases of prices, it should be noted that not all cases could be considered as evidence of tacit or other agreement. This is so, for example, in the case of parallel price increases that result from the increase in valued added tax, in which the prices of goods or services will rise in the same proportion and at the same time (comment transmitted by the Government of the Federal Republic of Germany).

60   Act No. LVII of 1996 on the Prohibition of Unfair and Restrictive Market Practices. Article 11 (2). (Hungary)

61   The law on Promotion of Competition and Restrictive Trading Practices. (Colombia)

62   Decree 2153 from 30 December 1992 on Functions of the Superintendency of Industry and Commerce. Article 47.

63   Decision 285 of the Commission of the Cartagena Agreement. Article 4 (f).

64   Northern Pacific Railway Co. v. United States, 356 US 1 (1958).

65   Information submitted by the Government of India.

66   In addition to the United States, a number of countries in recent amendments to their legislation have made price fixing and collusive tendering a per se prohibition.

67   Webb Pomerene Export Trade Act of 1918 and the 1982 Export Trading Company Act. It is to point out that United States Antitrust Law (through the Foreign Trade Antitrust Improvements Act of 1982, 15 U.S.C. Section 6 (a)) applies to anti competitive effects on United States export markets, and not merely on United States domestic markets. Also, joint ventures formed under the United States Export Trading Company Act cannot be described as "export cartels", because they do not possess market power in domestic or foreign markets; rather, they are export oriented joint ventures whose activities are circumscribed to ensure that they have no anti competitive effects on United States markets (Information provided by the United States Government).

68   Concerning export cartels, United States antitrust law (through the Foreign Trade Antitrust Improvements Act of 1982, 15 U.S.C. Section 6 (a)) applies to anti competitive effects on United States export markets and the domestic market. It should also be noted that joint ventures formed under the United States Export Trading Company Act cannot be described as "export cartels", because they do not possess market power in any United States domestic or foreign market; rather, they are export oriented joint ventures whose activities are carefully circumscribed to ensure that they have no anti competitive effects on United States markets (Comment transmitted by the Government of the United States).

69   See "Collusive tendering" study by the UNCTAD secretariat (TD/B/RBP/12).

[70]   Comment transmitted by the Commission of the European Community. The exemption rules on exclusive distribution agreements refer to Commission Regulation (EEC) No. 1983/83 on the Application of article 85 (3) of the Treaty of Rome to categories of exclusive distribution agreements. Official Journal L73, 30 June 1983, p. 1; Corrigendum OJ L281, 13 October 1983, p. 24.

[71]   The Associated Press (AP) v. United States exemplifies this point. 326 US, 165S Ct. 1416, 86L. Ed. 2013, rehearing denied 326 (802) 1945. For further details see: TD/B/RBP/15/Rev.1, para. 54.

[72]   Wilk v. American Medical Association, 1987, 2CCH Trade Cas. Section 67,721 (N.D. Ill. 1987).

[73]   As an example, the New York Stock Exchange (NYSE) ordered a number of its members to remove private direct telephone wire connections previously in operation between their offices and those of the non member, without giving the non member notice, assigning him any reason for the action, or affording him an opportunity to be heard. The plaintiff (a securities dealer) alleged that in violation of Sherman 1 and 2 the NYSE had conspired with its members firms to deprive him of the private wire communications and ticker service, and that the disconnection injured his business because of the inability to obtain stock quotations quickly, the inconvenience to other brokers in calling him and the stigma attached to the disconnection. The US Supreme Court stated that, in the absence of any justification derived from the policy of another statute or otherwise, the NYSE had acted in violation of the Sherman Act; that the Securities Exchange Act contained no express antitrust exemption to stock exchanges; and that the collective refusal to continue private wires occurred under totally unjustifiable circumstances and without according fair procedures. Silver v. New York Stock Exchange. 373 US 341, (1963). For further details see: *idem*, para. 55.

[74]   An alternative for using the expression "will produce net public benefit" in the last part of the proposed article, might be using "do not produce public harm". This way it will be possible to avoid unjustified burden of proof on firms and the result in pro competitive practices (Comment transmitted by the United States Government).

[75]   Comment transmitted by the Commission of the European Communities. The examples mentioned in article 85 (1) are: (a) directly or indirectly fix purchase or selling prices or any other trading conditions; (b) limit or control production, markets, technical development, or investment; (c) share markets or sources of supply; (d) apply dissimilar conditions to equivalent transactions with other trading parties, thereby placing them at a competitive disadvantage; (e) make the conclusion of contracts subject to acceptance by the other parties of supplementary obligations which, by their nature or according to commercial usage, have no connection with the subject of such contracts.

[76]   Spanish legislation on this matter was developed by special regulations. Royal Decree 157/1992 of 21 February 1992, developing Law 16/1989 of 17 July 1992.

[77]   Decree 2153 of 30 December 1992, on the Superintendency of Industry and Commerce. Article 49.

[78]   Act No. LVII of 1996 on the Prohibition of Unfair and Restrictive Market Practices. Article 17 (1). (Hungary)

[79]   Lituanian Law revision 2000 Section 54 of the Act.

[80]   Law of 30 May 1995 on Competition and the Limitation of Monopolistic Activity in Commodity Markets. Article 6 (3).

[81]   Law No. 188/1991 of 8 July 1991 on Protection of Economic Competition. Article 5. Information provided by the Government of the Slovak Republic.

[82]   Comment provided by the United States Government.

[83]   Comments provided by the Commission of European Communities.

84   Comments provided by Tunisian Government.

85   Comments provided by the Commission of European Communities.

86   It is necessary to distinguish between using market share purely as a jurisdictional hurdle as in the United Kingdom where the 25 per cent market share provides for the firm(s) to be investigated rather than presuming guilt, or a critical market share figure giving rise to automatic controls, such as in the Russian Federation, where firms with over 35 per cent share are requested to notify the competition authority, are placed on the "monopoly register" and are subject to an element of State oversight (Comment transmitted by the Government of the United Kingdom).

87   Law of 24 February 1990 on Counteracting Monopolistic Practices. Article 2 (7).

88   Decree Law No. 371/93 of 29 October 1993 on the Protection and Promotion of Competition. Article 3 (3) (a). (Czech Republic)

89   Law of Mongolia on Prohibiting Unfair Competition. Article 3 (1).

90   Information provided by the Government of Canada.

91   Law of 30 May 1995 on Competition and the Limitation of Monopolistic Activity in Commodity Markets. Article 4.

92   Act against Restraints of Competition, 1957, as amended. Section 19 (3).

93   Information provided by the Commission of the European Communities. Akzo Case, 3 July 1991.

94   The Competition and Fair Trading Act 1994 Section 7 (2).

95   Information provided by the Commission of the European Communities. Michelin Judgement, 9 November 1993.

96   CJE, 14 February 1978. United Brands Company and United Brands Continental BV v. Commission, 27/ 76, 1978, ECR 207. Companie Maritime Belge C-395/96 P and C – 396/96 P [2000] ECR I-1365; Airtours (Case T-349/99 [2002] ECR II -2585.

97   Comment transmitted by the Commission of the European Communities. Vetro Piano in Italia Judgement of 10 March 1992.

98   Information provided by the Commission of the European Communities. Decision "Nestlé Perrier" of 22 July 1992.

99   Information provided by the Government of the United Kingdom.

100   For additional information on United States Law (Supreme Court Decisions) on non price vertical restraints in distribution, see: White Motor Co. v. United States, 372 U.S. 253, 83 S.CT. 696, 9 L.Ed.2d 738 (1963) (applies the rule of reason); United States v. Arnold Schwinn & Co., 388 U.S. 365, 87 S.CT. 1856, 18 L.Ed.2d 1249 (1967) (applies the "per se" approach), and particularly, Continental T.V. Inc. v. GTE Sylvania Inc., 433 U.S. 36, 97 S.CT. 2549, 53 L.Ed.2d 568 (1977) (rejects the "per se" approach of Schwinn and returns to the rule of reason).

101   Law of 2 September 1993 of the People's Republic of China for Countering Unfair Competition. Article 11. This law also lists a number of cases not considered unfair such as, selling fresh goods, seasonal lowering of prices, changing the line of production or closing the business.

102   Law of Mongolia on Prohibiting Unfair Competition. Article 4 (3).

103 Act No. LVII of 1996 on the Prohibition of Unfair and Restrictive Market Practices. Article 21 (h). (Hungary)

104 McDonald v. Johnson and Johnson, No. 4 79 189 (D. Minn, 14 April 1982).

105 Hugin Liptons case. Commission Decision of 8 December 1977 (Official Journal of the European Communities, L.22 of 17 January 1978). Also, Instituto Chemioterapico Italiano S.P.S. Commercial Solvents: Judgement of 6 March 1974.

106 See: Effem and Atlas Building Products Company v. Diamond Block & Gravel Company cases.

107 See footnote 12. Legislative Decree 701 Against Monopolistic Control and Restriction Practices Affecting Free Competition 1992 Art. 5(b).

108 Trade Practices Act, 1974, Section 49, subsection 1.

109 Information provided by the Swedish Government.

110 Reference is made to the Consumer Protection Act 1987, where it is an offence to give a "misleading price indication". When considering whether or not a particular price indication is misleading, the parties can refer to a statutory Code of Conduct approved by the Secretary of State in 1988. Paragraph 1.6.3 (c) advises traders not to use a recommended price in a comparison unless "the price is not significantly higher than prices at which the product is genuinely sold at the time you first made the comparison". In other words, a dealer who says "Recommended Retail Price XXX Pounds, my Price is half less", may be regarded as giving a misleading price indication and thus committing a criminal offence under the Consumer Protection Act if that recommended retail price is significantly higher than the prices at which the goods are usually sold by other dealers.

111 The Competition Act, 1985, Section 61 (4).

112 Official Journal of the European Communities, No. L.377/16 of 31 December 1980.

113 FTC Decision of 18 April 1978. Information transmitted by the Government of Japan.

114 Cinzano and Cie. GmbH v. Jara Kaffee GmbH and Co. Decision of 2 February 1973.

115 Tepea B.V. v. E.C. Commission, Case 28/77; Commission decision of 21 December 1976. The Commission's decision was upheld by the European Court of Justice in its ruling of 24 June 1978.

116 Judgement given on 10 October 1978, Case 3/78: (1978) ECR 1823.

117 Decisions "Tetra Pak" of 22 July 1991 and "Hilti" of 22 December 1987. They were confirmed by, respectively, the Court of First Instance Judgement of 6 October 1994, and Judgement of the Court of Justice of the European Communities of 2 March 1994.

118 Comment provided by the United States Government.

119 Concerning unilateral refusals to deal, see: United States v. Colgate & Co., Supreme Court of the United States, 1919. 250 U.S. 300, 39 S.CT. 465, 53 1.Ed. 992, 7 A.L.R. 443. Also: Eastman Kodak V. Image Technical Services, Inc, 504 US 451(1992) (holding that a monopolistic right to refuse to deal with a competitor is not absolute, the jury should be permitted to decide if the defendant's proffered reasons were pretextual).

120 In the United States, tying arrangements have been found unlawful where sellers exploit their market power over one product to force unwilling buyers into acquiring another. See Jefferson Parish Hospital District No.2 V. Hyde, 466 V.S.2, 12(1984); Northern Pac. Ry Co. V. United States, 356 US1, 6 (1958); Times – Picayune Pub. Co. V. United States, 345 US 594, 605 (1953). Liability for tying under section one of the Sherman Act exists where (i) two separate products are involved; (ii) the defendent affords its customers no choice but to take the tied product in order to obtain the tying product; (iii) the arrangement affects a

substantial volume of interstate commerce; and (iv) the defendant has "market power" in the tying product market. Jefferson Parish Hospital District No.2 V. Hyde, 466 US.2 (1984) Eastman Kodak Co. V. Image Technical Services, Inc 504 US. 451, 461-62 (1992). The United States Supreme Court had defined tying arrangements as: "an agreement by a party to sell one product but only on the condition that the buyer also purchase a different (or tied) product, or at least agrees that he will not purchase that product from any other supplier". Northern Pac. Ry. v. United States, 356 U.S. 1, 5 6, 78 S.CT. 514, 518, 2 L.Ed.ed 545 (1958). Also it has stated that: "the usual tying contract forces the customer to take a product or brand he does not necessarily want in order to secure one which he does desire. Because such an arrangement is inherently anti competitive, we (the Supreme Court) have held that its use by an established company is likely "substantially to lessen competition" although a relatively small amount of commerce is affected." Brown Shoe Co. v. United States, 370 U.S. 294, 330, 82 S.CT. 1502, 1926, 8 L.Ed. 2d 510 (1962).

121   For a discussion of tied purchasing in its various forms and the legal situation in various countries, see: UNCTAD, "Tied purchasing" (TD/B/RBP/18).

122   Ordinance No. 95 06 of 25 January 1995 on Competition. Article 7.

123   Act No. LVII of 1996 on the Prohibition of Unfair and Restrictive Market Practices. Article 21 (f).

124   Law of Mongolia on Prohibiting Unfair Competition. Article 4 (5).

125   Federal Law on Cartels and other Restrictions to Competition of 6 October 1995. (cart, RS 251, FF 1995 I 472. Article 7 (f)).

126   MERCOSUR/CMC/No. 21/94, Decision on protection of competition. Annex, article 4 (d).

127   See footnote 88.

128   See footnote 39.

129   So far, merger control has been presented in the Model Law as in the Set, under the concept of "abuse of dominant position". In line with modern competition legislation, a separate provision for merger control is now proposed in the Model Law.

130   The Competition and Fair Trading Act 1994. (Zambia)

131   The Competition Act 2002 Section (2). (India)

132   The Competition and Fair Trading Act 1994. (Zambia)

133   The Competition Act 1996. (Zimbabwe)

134   Information provided by the Commission of the European Communities. Council Regulation (EEC) No. 4064/89 of 21 December 1989 on the control of concentrations between undertakings (OJ L395, 30 December 1989), p. 1. In particular article 1.

135   Council Regulation (EEC) No. 4064/89 of December 1989 on the control of concentrations between undertakings (OJ L 395, 30 December 1989) as amended by Council Regulation (EC) No. 1310 97 (OJ L 180, 9 July 1997).

136   For a detailed analysis of the concentration of market power through mergers, takeovers, joint ventures and other acquisitions of control, and its effects on international markets, in particular the markets of developing countries, see TD/B/RBP/80/Rev.1.

137   Provisions concerning the referral to the competent authorities of the member States are considered in article 9 of Council Regulation 4064/89.

138   Provisions concerning the referral by the competent authorities of the member States of an operation for consideration to the European Commission are included in article 22 of Council Regulation 4064/89.

139   For example, the Korean Fair Trade Office held illegal an acquisition combining a Company with 54 per cent of the PVC stabilizer market and another company with 19 per cent of the same market. The acquiring company was ordered to dispose of the stock. In re Dong Yang Chemical Industrial Co., 1 KFTC 153. 13 January 1982.

140   See footnote 18.

141   Comments provided by the Australian Government.

142   Under the United States experience, conglomerate mergers are highly unlikely to pose competitive problems (comment submitted by the United States Government). In the United Kingdom, it is unlikely that the merger would be referred if there were no overlap in any market (comment transmitted by the Government of the United Kingdom).

143   Cf. Order of the Ministry of Economy, Finance and Industry of 4 July 2001, after the opinion rendered by the Competition Council on 12 June 2001 (cf. www.concentrations.mienfi.gouv.fr).

144   The United States firm Gillette acquired 100 per cent of Wilkinson Sword, a United Kingdom company, with the exception of the European Union and United States based activities. Because of merger control regulations in the European Union and the United States, Gillette had so far acquired only a 22.9 per cent non voting capital participation in Eemland Holding N.V., a Netherlands firm and sole shareholder of Wilkinson Sword Europe, accompanied, however, by additional agreements providing for a competitively significant influence on Eemland and consequently also on Wilkinson Sword Europe. Gillette and Wilkinson are the worldwide largest manufacturers of wet shaving products, including razor blades and razors, the relevant product market as defined by all authorities involved. Although the market shares of both firms varied from country to country, they held in most relevant geographical markets the two leading positions. In many West European countries, Gillette and Wilkinson accounted for a combined market share of around 90 per cent. In March 1993, Eemland disposed of its Wilkinson Sword business to Warner Lambert and retransferred the trademarks and business in various non EU countries. The transactions described led to the initiation of competition proceedings in 14 jurisdictions worldwide. The case illustrates particularly well the problems which can be raised by international cases owing to the fact that they may cause competitive effects in many countries and consequently lead to as many competition proceedings under different laws. For the enterprises concerned, as well as for the administrations involved, such cases may imply an extremely costly operation in terms of human and financial resources. Obviously, these problems would not exist if such cases could be dealt with under one law by one authority. As such authority does not exist, close cooperation among the competition authorities appears to be in the interest of both the participating firms and the competition authorities involved. For additional cases, see: Restrictive business practices that have an effect in more than one country, in particular developing and other countries, with overall conclusions regarding the issues raised by these cases (UNCTAD TD/RBP/CONF.4/6).

145   Note that under United Kingdom law, interlocking directorships, alone, would not give rise to a merger situation. Interlocking directorship without substantial cross share holdings are more likely to give rise to restrictive agreements than mergers. Comment submitted by the Government of the United Kingdom.

146   The situation has to be considered not only at the level of directors. In the United States, Section 8 of the Clayton Act prohibits a person from serving as a director or board-elected or appointed officer of two or more corporations if (i) the combined capital, surplus, and undivided profit of each of the corporations is more than $10 million (adjusted for inflation) (ii) each corporation is engaged in whole or in part in commerce; and (iii) the corporations are "competitor", or that an agreement between them would violate any of the antitrust Laws. 15 U.S.C 19 (a)(1)(B). There are several exceptions to Section 8 to ensure that arrangements that

pose little risk of significant injury are not covered (e.g. the competitive sales of each company are less than 2 per cent of that company's total sales).

147   N. MUHAMMAD, *"Promoting Competition in Regulated Sectors or State Enterprises and the Role of Government on Monopoly Practices in Indonesia"*. Fifth APEC/PFP Course on Competition Policy, Bangkok, March 2001.

148   A recent OECD roundtable, organized by the Committee on Competition Law and Policy, has shown that specific regulatory regimes can also be found in radio and television broadcasting, cable television, civil aviation, ocean shipping, pharmaceuticals, banking, inter-city bus transportation and trucking, etc. See OECD, "The relationship between competition and regulatory authorities", *OECD Journal of Competition Law and Policy*, Paris, 1999, vol. 1, no.3, p. 169- 246. See also the papers produced for a recent Inter-American Development Bank symposium, held in Washington, DC, in April 2001, on competition policy issues in infrastructure industries.

149   These network effects or "network externalities", often arise in information and communication technology industries. There are often benefits derived from being on a larger network, or on a more widely adopted standard, as it increases the number of people with whom one can interact or conduct economic transactions. Provided there are costs of being connected to (or compatible with) two or more networks (or standards), consumers will pay more for being on a larger network. Markets which exhibit sizeable network externalities may only be able to sustain a single firm. These facts emerge from studies by the OECD Committee on Competition Law and Policy in connection with the elaboration of an OECD recommendation on the separation of vertically integrated industries, which was drafted in 2000. See in particular OECD, *Structural Separation in Regulated Industries*, Paris, 2000.

150   See I. De Leon, *The Role of Competition Policy in the Regulation of Infrastructure Industries: Some Lessons from the Latin American Experience*. Washington, DC, *Inter-American Development Bank* Working Paper, 2001.

151   R.G. Maru, Promoting Competition in Regulated Sectors or State Enterprises in Papua New Guinea. Fifth APEC/PFP Course on Competition Policy, Bangkok, 2001.

152   It has recently been stressed that in the case of developing countries in South America, competition institutions very often do not have the power to impose penalties or to overrule the regulatory authorities' decision. "When immunity from competition law enforcement is provided for regulated firms, there is no assurance that they will be properly regulated in this respect, should a case arise, as regulatory agencies lack the expertise in handling competition regulation. In these cases, when conduct is detected, and no competition authority intervenes (as a result of the immunity from competition law enforcement), there are no legal powers granted to the regulatory agency to intervene." This is the case, for example, of Colombia's as well as Argentina's Regulatory Commission for Energy, "which detected abusive behavior among gas producers, but could not intervene". De Leon, op. cit., p.3.

153   Among many statements, see Chul Ho Ji, *Promotion of Competition in State-owned Enterprises (SOEs) and Regulated Sectors in Korea*. Fifth APEC/PFP Course on Competition Policy, Bangkok, 2001.

154   See in particular OECD, *Report on Regulatory Reform*, vols. I and II, Paris, 1997. With regard to developing countries and countries in transition, see D. Zemanovicova, *Regulatory Barriers to Economic Competition in Transitional Countries,* Bratislava, 1998 (published under the Phare-ACE programme).

155   See, for instance, OECD, *Antitrust and Market Access: The Scope and Coverage of Competition Laws and Implications for Trade*, Paris, 1996.

156   This paragraph and the following developments, including box 15 on the submission of local governments to competition review in the European Union have been included in this document at the repeated request of the Russian Federation in sessions of the IGE on Competition Law and policy in 2000 and 2001.

[157] The EU policy of liberalization is rooted in a number of texts called "directives". The main legal texts incorporating the notion of services of general interest as well as provisions on competition preserving the general interest are the following: Council Directive concerning the co-ordination of procedures for the award of public works contracts 71/305/EEC, OJEC 1971, L185/5, as amended by Directive 89/440/EEC, OJCE 1989, L210/1 and codified by Directive 93/37 OJEC 1993, L 199; Council Directive 77/62/EEC concerning the co-ordination of procedures for the award of public supply contracts, OJEC 1977/ L 13/1, codified by Directive 93/96 EEC, OJEC 1993 L 199; Council Directive 89/665/EEC on the co-ordination of the laws, regulations and administrative provisions relating to the application of review procedures for the award of public supply and public work contracts, OJEC 1989, L 395/33, modified by Directive 92/50 OJEC 1992, L 209; Council Directive 90/531/EEC on the procurement procedures of entities operating in water, energy, transports and telecommunications sectors, OJEC 1990, L297/1, codified by Directive 93/38, OJEC 1993 L 199; Council Directive 92/13/EEC co-ordinating the laws, regulations and administrative provisions relating to the application of Community rules on the procurement procedures of entities operating in water, energy, transports and telecommunications sectors, OJEC 1992 L 76/14; Council Directive 92/50/EEC relating to the co-ordination of procedures for the award of public services contracts, OJEC 1992, L 209/1. Furthermore, to define what is meant by "general interest", the European Commission explained in its Guidelines in 1996 that the extension of competition rules would not run counter to obligations of public service that might be imposed by the public authorities on the entities — public or private — that perform services for protection of economic and social cohesion, the environment, the planning and promotion of consumers interests, and land use. See EU Commission, *Communication on Services of General Interest in Europe,* Brussels, September 1996.

[158] See for instance OECD, *Review of Regulatory Reform in Spain*, Paris, OECD, 2000, p. 164.

[159] General Assembly resolution 39/248 of 9 April 1995.

[160] Id. Section 15.

[161] The Monopolies and Restrictive Trade Practices Ordinance (amended), June 1980.

[162] Decree 2153 of 30 December 1992, on the Superintendency of Industry and Commerce. Article 3. The Superintendency is also responsible for the administration of the following legislation: patents, trademarks, consumer protection, chambers of commerce, technical standards and metrology.

[163] Decree Law No. 25868. Law creating the National Institute for the Safeguard of Competition and the Protection of Intellectual Property (INDECOPI). Article 2. INDECOPI is also responsible for the administration of the following legislation: dumping and subsidies, consumer protection, advertising, unfair competition, metrology, quality control and non custom barriers, bankruptcy procedures, trademarks, patents, plant varieties, appellations of origin and transfer of technology.

[164] Law 22.262 for the Safeguarding of Competition. Article 7.

[165] Decree 511 from 27 October 1980. Reference to Legislative Decree 2.760. Article 16.

[166] Decree 511 from 27 October 1980. Reference to Legislative Decree 2.760. Article 16 and Legislative Decree No. 701 Against Monopolistic, Controlist and Restrictive Practices Affecting Free Competition, 1992. Article 10.

[167] The Competition and Fair Trading Act 1994 Section 4.

[168] Federal Law n° 8884 of 1994 on the Competition Defense System.

[169] Act No. LVII of 1996 on the Prohibition of Unfair and Restrictive Market Practices. Article 38 (3) (d).

[170] Price Fixing and Anti Monopoly Act, B.E. 2522 (1979). Section 12 (6).

171   Comments provided by the Government of United Kingdom.

172   Federal Law on Economic Competition.

173   Act No. LVII of 1996 on the Prohibition of Unfair and Restrictive Market Practices.

174   Law of 2 September 1993 of the People's Republic of China for Countering Unfair Competition. Article 32.

175   Comment provided by the Government of Panama.

176   Decree Law No. 371/93 of 29 October 1993 on the Protection and Promotion of Competition. Articles 13 (1) (c) and 13 (2). (Portugal)

177   Ordinance 86 1243 of 1 December 1986 on the Liberalization of Prices and Competition. Article 44.

178   Statute of 15 November 1991 on the Organization and Activities of the Commission for the Protection of Competition. Article 4 (3).

179   Decree Law No. 371/93 of 29 October 1993 on Protection and Promotion of Competition. Article 13 (1) (b), (c) and (d).

180   Law 16/1989 of 17 July for the Protection of Competition. Article 26. Additional information on this matter can be found at: Tribunal de Defensa de la Competencia. Memoria 1992, p. 66.

181   Law on the Safeguarding of Economic Competition. Article 50 (b).

182   Federal Law on Economic Competition, 1992. Article 31, para. 2; and Internal Rules of the Federal Commission for Competition of 12 October 1993. Article 4.

183   Decree Law No. 371/93 of 29 October 1993 on Protection and Promotion of Competition. Article 19.

184   Federal Law on Cartels and other Restrictions on Competition of 6 October 1995 (Cart. RS 251, FF 1995 I 472. Article 25).

185   Legislative Decree No. 701 Against Monopolistic, Controlist and Restrictive Practices Affecting Free Competition, 1992. Article 23 (Information provided by the Peruvian Government).

186   Information provided by the Commission of the European Communities.

187   Antitrust Amendment Act of 1990.

188   Information provided by the United States Government.

189   Act No. LVII of 1996 on the Prohibition of Unfair and Restrictive Market Practices. Article 72 (1) (c) and 72 (2).

190   In re Samsung Electronics Company, 4 KFTC 58. 26 December 1984.

191   Ordinance 86 1243 of 1 December 1986 on Liberalization of Prices and Competition. Articles 12 and 15.

192   Federal Law on Economic Competition, 1992. Article 35 (I).

193   Information provided by the Government of the United States. It is to be noted that in the United States, divestiture is considered as a "structural remedy", requiring some dismantling or sale of the corporate structure or property which contributed to the continuing restraint of trade, monopolization or acquisition. Structural relief can be subdivided into three categories known as the "Three Ds": dissolution, divestiture and divorcement. "Dissolution" is generally used to refer to a situation where the dissolving of an allegedly illegal combination or association is involved; it may include the use of divestiture and divorcement as methods of achieving that end. "Divestiture" refers to situations where the defendants are required to divest themselves of property,

securities or other assets. "Divorcement" is a term commonly used to indicate the effect of a decree where certain types of divestiture are ordered; it is especially applicable to cases where the purpose of the proceeding is to secure relief against antitrust abuses flowing from integrated ownership or control (such as vertical integration of manufacturing and distribution functions or integration of production and sale of diversified products unrelated in use or function). This type of remedy is not created in express terms by statute. But Section 4 of the Sherman Act and Section 5 of the Clayton Act empower the Attorney General to institute proceedings in equity to "prevent and restrain violations of the antitrust laws", and provide that "Such proceedings may be by way of petition setting forth the case and praying that such violation shall be enjoined otherwise prohibited". Further, aside from these general statutory authorizations, the essence of equity jurisdiction is the power of the court to mould the decree to the necessities of the particular case. Thus, invocation by the Government of the general authority of a court of equity under Sherman or Clayton Acts enables the court to exercise wide discretion in framing its decree so as to give effective and adequate relief. Chesterfield Oppenheim, Weston and McCarthy, Federal Antitrust Laws, West Publishing Co., 1981, pp. 1042 43. See also, A study of the Commission 's Divesture Process, Bureau of Competitoin of the Federal Trade Commission, 1999, available at http://www.ftc.gov/os/1999/9908/divestiture/pdf.

194   Comment submitted by the Government of the United Kingdom.

195   Law on Competition, 1992. Article 14 concerning appeals against decisions of the Institution of Price and Competition. It is to point out that the law establishes that appeals to court shall not suspend compliance with directions and decisions, unless the court stipulates otherwise.

196   Law of 30 May 1995 on Competition and the Limitation of Monopolistic Activity in Commodity Markets. Article 28 on procedure for appealing against decisions of the Anti Monopoly Committee.

197   Law on Promotion of Competition and restrictive Commercial Practices. (Colombia)

198   Decree Law No. 371/93 of 29 October 1993 on Protection and Promotion of Competition. Articles 28 and 35.

199   Section 62 of the Competition Act, 1993. Only in those cases mentioned in Sections 60 and 61 of the Act may decisions taken by the Swedish Competition Authority be appealed to the Market Court.

200   Law of 30 May 1995 on Competition and the Limitation of Monopolistic Activity in Goods Markets, article 28.

201   Trade Practices Tribunal.

202   Appeal Tribunal appointed by the Minister of Commerce.

203   Restrictive Trade Practices Tribunal.

204   Tribunal for the Defence of Competition and Intellectual Property.

205   Court for the Protection of Competition.

206   See the Hart Scott Rodino Antitrust Improvement Act of 1976, with respect to the United States.

207   Federal Law on Economic Competition, 1992, article 38.

208   Legislative Decree Against Monopolistic, Control and Restrictive Practices Affecting Free Competition. Article 25.

209   Law to Promote and Protect the Exercise of Free Competition. Article 55.

ANNEXES

ANNEX I

Names of competition laws around the world

Several countries adopted competition laws in the 1980s, 1990s and 2000; Below are examples of names given to these laws by countries, in alphabetical order.

Country	Name of the competition law
Algeria	Law on the Safeguarding of Economic Competition
Argentina	Law No. 22 262 of 1980 on Competition
Armenia	Law of the 6 of November 2000 on the Protection of Economic Competition
Australia	Trade Practices Act 1974
Austria	Cartel Act of 1998
Belgium	Law of 5 August 1991 on the Protection of Economic Competition
Brazil	Federal Law No. 8 884 of 1994 on the Competition Defense System
Canada	Competition Act
Chile	Antimonopoly Law
China	Antimonopoly Law
Colombia	Law on Promotion of Competition and Restrictive Commercial Practices
Costa Rica	Law on the Promotion of Competition and Effective Consumer Protection
Côte d'Ivoire	Law on Competition
Czech Republic	Commercial Competition Protection Act
Denmark	Competition Act 1997
Estonia	Competition Act
European Union	Rules of Competition of the Treaty instituting the European Community
Finland	Act on Restrictions on Competition
France	Ordinance No. 86 1243 of 1 December 1986 on Liberalization of Prices and Competition
Germany	Act Against Restraints of Competition of 1957
Greece	Law 703/77 on the Control of Monopolies and Oligopolies and Protection of Free Competition
Hungary	Act No LVII of 1996 on the Prohibition of Unfair and Restrictive Market Practices
India	The Competition Act 2002
Ireland	Competition Act 1991 and Mergers and Takeovers (Control) Acts 1978 to 1996; Competition Act 2002
Israel	Restraint of Trade Law, 5748 1988
Italy	Act No. 287/1990, "Rules for the Protection of Competition and the Market"
Jamaica	Fair Competition Act
Japan	Act Concerning the Prohibition of Private Monopolization and Maintenance of Fair Trade also called "Antimonopoly Law"
Kenya	The Restrictive Trade Practices, Monopolies and Trade Control Act
Luxembourg	Law of 17 June 1970 governing Restrictive Commercial Practices
Lithuania	Law on competition 1999

Country	Name of the competition law
Malta	Act to Regulate Competition and Provide for Fair Trading
Mexico	Federal Law on Economic Competition
Mongolia	Law on Prohibiting Unfair Competition
Netherlands	Competition Act of 22 May 1997
New Zealand	Commerce Act 1986
Norway	Competition Act of 1993
Pakistan	The Monopolies and Restrictive Trade Practices (Control and Prevention) Ordinance
Panama	Law on the Protection of Competition
Peru	Legislative Decree Against Monopolistic, Control and Restrictive Practices Affecting Free Competition
Poland	Law of Counteracting Monopolistic Practices Act of 24 February 1990
Portugal	Decree Law No. 371/93 of 29 October 1993 on the Protection and Promotion of Competition
Republic of Korea	Monopoly Regulation and Fair Trade Act of 1980
Russian Federation	Act on Competition and the Limitation of Monopolistic Monopoly Activity in Commodity Markets
Slovakia	Act No. 188/1994 Coll. on the Protection of Economic Competition Act No. 136/2001 Coll. on Protection of Competition Act No. 465/2002 Coll. on Block Exemptions from the Ban of Agreements Restricting Competition
South Africa	The Competition Act (Act No. 35 of 2000)
Spain	Law 16/1989 on the Defense of Competition Protection of Competition Law
Sri Lanka	The Fair Trading Commission Act
Sweden	Competition Act of 1993
Switzerland	Federal Law on Cartels and other Restrictions in Competition
Ukraine	Law of the 11th of January 2001 on the Protection of Economic Competition
United Kingdom	Fair Trading Act 1973, Competition Act 1980, Competition Act 1989, Enterprise Act 2002"
United States of America	Antitrust Laws (Sherman Act, Clayton Act, Federal Trade Commission Act, Hart Scott Rodino Antitrust Improvements Act)
Venezuela	Law to Promote and Protect the Exercise of Free Competition
Zambia	Competition and the Fair Trading Act, 1994
Zimbabwe	The Competition Act 1996
Bulgaria	Law on the protection of competition 1998

ANNEX II

Worldwide antitrust merger notification systems

Mandatory preclosing notification system		Mandatory postclosing notification system	Voluntary notification system
Albania	Kenya	Argentina	Australia
Argentina	Latvia	Greece	Chile
Austria	Lithuania	Indonesia (as of March 2000)	Côte d'Ivoire
Azerbaijan	Macedonia	Japan	India
Belarus	Mexico	Republic of Korea	New Zealand
Belgium	Republic of Moldova	Russian Federation	Norway
Brazil	Netherlands	South Africa	Panama
Bulgaria	Poland	Spain	United Kingdom
Canada	Portugal	The Former Yugoslav Republic of Macedonia	Venezuela
Colombia	Romania	Tunisia	
Croatia	Russia		
Cyprus	Slovak Republic		
Czech Republic	Slovenia		
Denmark	South Africa		
EU	South Korea		
Estonia	Sweden		
Finland	Switzerland		
France	Taiwan Province Of China		
Germany	Thailand		
Greece	Tunisia		
Hungary	Turkey		
Ireland	Ukraine		
Israel	United States		
Italy	Uzbekistan		
Japan	Yugoslavia		
Kazakhstan			

Source: UNCTAD Handbook on competition legislation.

ANNEX III

A selection of merger-control systems

1. Countries with mandatory preclosing notification system

Countries	Notification trigger/filing deadline	Clearance deadlines (Stage 1/Stage 2)	Substantive test for clearance	Penalties	Remarks
Brazil					
Mandatory system	Resulting market share at least 20 per cent in the relevant market or worldwide turnover over 400 million reales.

Filing should be made within 15 working days after execution of the transaction. | 30 days at SEA + 30 days at SDE + 60 days at CADE, interrupted every time the authorities issue official letters asking for further information.

No suspension effects. | Transactions which injure or limit competition will only be cleared if they result in efficiencies, and such efficiencies benefit consumers. | Failure to file: penalties may range from 55 000 reales to 5.5 million reales. | Regulated sectors are also subject to special rules. |
| **Canada** | | | | | |
| Mandatory system. | Merger pre notification is mandatory if statutory ownership asset and sales thresholds are exceeded.

The parties may file at any time after they have an agreement in principle, provided that sufficient information is available to complete the form. | A 14 or 42 day waiting period, depending on whether a short or long form filing is elected (subject to the right of the Commissioner to extend the period in the case of a short form). In rare circumstances, a waiting period can be abridged by the Director. Suspension during waiting periods. | Whether the merger will or is likely to prevent or lessen competition substantially in a relevant market. | The failure to notify a pre notifiable transaction is a criminal offence subject to a fine of up to C$ 50 000. | Transactions involving non Canadians may be notified under the Investment Canada Act, and may be notifiable under the notification provisions of the *Competition Act* if its thresholds are exceeded. Media, insurance company, loan company and bank mergers, among others, may be subject to notification and review under industry specific legislation. |
| **Colombia** | | | | | |
| Mandatory system. | Companies carrying on the same activities, e.g. production, supply, distribution, or consumption of a given article, raw material, product, merchandise, or service, whose assets, either individually or jointly, are at least 20 million pesos (approximately US$ 10 000) must notify all consolidation and/or merger projects. | The Superintendent has 30 banking days from the date of submission of the information to reject the proposed merger. If within that time the Superintendent does not respond, the merger may proceed. | Whether competition is unduly restricted by the merger. | If all legal requirements are not met, the merger will be considered null and void. | A Constitutional Court ruling that Decree 1122 of 1999 is unconstitutional is a setback for merger control in Colombia; it is expected that the regulations contained in Decree 1122 will be re enacted in the near future, as the Court decision was procedurally flawed. |

Countries	Notification trigger/filing deadline	Clearance deadlines (Stage 1/Stage 2)	Substantive test for clearance	Penalties	Remarks
European Union					
European Merger Control Regulation. Mandatory system. Form of notification: Special form: Form CO. Detailed information on the parties (turnover, business sectors, groups), the merger proposal, the affected markets, competitors and customers. In any of the EU official languages.	Combined worldwide turnover over 5 billion euros and EU wide turnover of at least two parties over 250 million euros unless each of the parties achieves more than 2/3 of the EU turnover in one and the same State or combined worldwide turnover over 2.5 billion euros; EU wide turnover of at least two of the undertakings over 100 million euros each; combined turnover in each of at least three member States over 100 million euros; a turnover in each of those three member States by each of at least two of the undertakings over 25 million euros unless each of the parties achieves more than 2/3 of the EU turnover in one and the same State. Pre merger filing, within one week of conclusion of agreement or announcement of public bid or acquisition of control (whichever is earliest).	Stage 1: one month from notification or six weeks from notification where the parties have submitted commitments intended to form the basis of a clearance decision. Stage 2: four additional months. Suspension effects: suspension of transaction until final decision with limited exception for public bids.	Whether a merger will create or strengthen a dominant position which will significantly impede competition in the common market or a substantial part of it. In addition, the cooperative aspects of full function joint ventures are appraised in accordance with the criteria of article 81(1) and (3). Broadly, economic benefits must outweigh detriment to competition.	Failure to file: fines from 1 000 to 50 000 euros. Implementation before clearance: fines up to 10 per cent of the combined worldwide turnover of the parties.	Special rules for the calculation of thresholds for banks and insurance companies. Mergers in the coal and steel sectors are subject to the Coal and Steel Treaty (notice on alignment of procedures adopted on 1 March 1998).
Germany					
New legislation in force as of January 1999. Mandatory system. Form of notification: no special form; shorter than Form CO; in German.	Combined worldwide turnover of all parties over DM 1 billion and at least one party with a turnover of at least DM 50 million in Germany (de minimis exemptions). Pre merger notification any time before completion.	Stage 1: one month from notification. Stage 2: three additional months. Suspension effects: prohibition to complete before clearance (possibility of exemption for important reasons).	Whether a merger will create or strengthen a dominant market position (statutory presumptions of dominance) which is not outweighed by an improvement in market conditions.	Failure to notify; incomplete, incorrect or late notification: fines of up to DM 50 000. Completion before clearance: fines of up to DM 1 million or three times additional revenues; transaction invalid. Failure to submit post completion notice: fines of up to DM 50 000.	Special provisions in the broadcasting sector. Further notification procedures for banks and insurance companies. Post completion notice without "undue delay" after completion of the merger notified.
India					
Mandatory system.	Companies Act: share acquisitions exceeding 25 per cent; transfer of assets exceeding 10 per cent. Takeover Code: share acquisitions of 10 per cent or more.	Companies Act: shares of foreign companies: 60 days. No other deadlines.	Interest of company or public interest or interest of shareholders.	Failure to implement: Penalties provided.	Special provisions for foreign companies with established business in India.

Countries	Notification trigger/filing deadline	Clearance deadlines (Stage 1/Stage 2)	Substantive test for clearance	Penalties	Remarks
Italy					
Mandatory system. Form of notification: special form. Detailed information similar to Form CO. In Italian.	Combined aggregate turnover realized in Italy of all the undertakings concerned exceeds 387 million euros, or if the aggregate turnover realized in Italy of the undertaking, which is to be acquired, exceeds 39 million of euros. The thresholds are updated each year by an amount equivalent to the increase of the GDP price deflator. Pre merger filing, any time before completion.	Stage 1: 30 days from notification. 15 days from notification of a public takeover bid Stage 2: 45 additional days (extendable by a further 30 days where insufficient information). No suspension effects. As a general rule, transaction can be implemented after notification. Suspension effects: when conducting the investigation, the Italian Competition Authority may order the suspension of transaction until final decision with limited exception for public takeover bids".	Whether the merger will create or strengthen a dominant position in the national market in a way that threatens to eliminate or reduce competition to a considerable and lasting extent.	Failure to file: fines up to 1 per cent of parties' turnover in Italy in the year preceding the statement of objections. Implementation before clearance: no penalties. Failure to comply with the prohibition on concentration requirements: fines from a minimum of one per cent to a maximum of ten per cent of the turnover of the business forming the object of the concentration and if the concentration has already taken place the Authority may require measures to be taken in order to restore conditions of effective competition, and remove any effects that distort it.	Special provisions in film distribution sectors and for banks.
Japan					
Mandatory system. Form of notification: filing of formal report to the Fair Trade Commission (FTC). Notification must be submitted in Japanese.	Amendments to the law, which became effective on 1 January 1999, have relaxed the requirements for merger and business transfer filings by establishing monetary thresholds. Under these amendments, only mergers and business transfers between a company having total assets of more than ¥ 10 billion and a company having total assets of more than ¥ 1 billion will be subject to a filing requirement.	No company shall consummate a merger or business transfer until after the expiration of a 30 day waiting period, which runs from the date that the FTC formally accepts the merger or business transfer notification, in the absence of any objection from the FTC.	Clearance will be given if the merger's or business transfer's effect does not substantially restrain competition in the relevant market.	Failure to file: maximum fine of ¥ 2 million. Implementation before clearance: maximum fine of ¥ 2 million.	A revenue threshold applies to the acquisition of a new Japanese company.

Countries	Notification trigger/filing deadline	Clearance deadlines (Stage 1/Stage 2)	Substantive test for clearance	Penalties	Remarks
Mexico					
Mandatory system. Written file and form for notification. The form is completed partially if it is clear that there are no effects on markets, and in full if it is necessary to evaluate concentration in markets. The written file and form must be completed in Spanish.	Normal procedure: about 40 calendar days, may be extended up to 145 in complex cases. Notification before the mergers are effected. A concentration must be notified if it reaches any of the following thresholds: (i) If the transaction, in one act or successive acts, amounts to more than the equivalent of 12 million times the current general minimum wage for the Federal District; (ii) If the transaction, in one act or successive acts, amounts to 35 per cent or more of the assets or shares of an economic agent with assets or sales equivalent to more than 12 million times the current general minimum wage for the Federal District; or (iii) If the transaction includes the participation of two or more economic agents with assets or an annual turnover jointly or separately totalling more than 48 million times the current general minimum wage for the Federal District, and the transaction involves additional combined assets or equity capital equivalent to more than 4,800,000 times the current general minimum wage for the Federal District. Notification must be made before completion of the concentration.	(1) Acquisition of a target worth about US\$ 44 million or more; (2) Acquisition of 35 per cent or more of a firm with assets or sales of over US\$ 176 million or more, including the acquisition of assets or shares of stock of or over US\$ 18 million. Essentially assets or sales within Mexico. The period for clearance is 45 calendar days as from the time of completion of the notification. Filing is understood to have been completed when the agents submit the information required from them by the Commission. The period of 45 calendar days may be extended.	General: lessening, harming or prevention of competition. Specific: acquisition of market power, displacement of competitors or market foreclosure; facilitating anti competitive (per se or rule of reason) practices. It must be indicated that the agent engaged in concentration is not acquiring or strengthening substantial power in the relevant market; in addition, it must be indicated that the agent is not acquiring the capacity to implement anti-competitive practices.	Failure to file: fines (up to US\$ 300 000) and transaction null and void. Fine up to the equivalent of 225,000 times the current general minimum wage for the Federal District, for engaging in any concentration prohibited by the law; and up to the equivalent of 100,000 times the current general minimum wage for the Federal District for failure to notify the concentration when legally bound to do so.	Competition rules govern most specially regulated areas. Special rules for banks and telecommunications. Subject to the law are all economic agents, whether natural or legal persons, branches or entities of the federal, state or municipal public administration, associations, groupings of professionals, trustees or any other form of participation in the economic activity.

Countries	Notification trigger/filing deadline	Clearance deadlines (Stage 1/Stage 2)	Substantive test for clearance	Penalties	Remarks
Portugal					
Mandatory system.	Combined market share in Portugal greater than 30 per cent or combined turnover in Portugal of over 30 billion escudos. Filing: before the legal transactions putting the concentration into effect are concluded and before the announcement of any public bid relating thereto.	Stage 1: 40 days as of notification (extendable by information request or if false information is notified) or 90 days if the authorities initiate the procedure ex officio. The file is sent to the Minister in charge of trade matters for decision. Stage 2: Within 50 or up to 95 days of notification, depending on a positive or negative assessment of the operation. Suspension until clearance.	Whether the operation creates or reinforces a dominant position in Portugal, or in a substantial part of Portugal, which is liable to prevent, distort or restrict competition. However, the transaction may be authorized if (1) the economic balance of the envisaged merger is positive or (2) the international competitiveness of the participating undertakings is significantly increased.	Failure to file: fines ranging from 100 000 to 100 million escudos. Implementation before clearance: the transaction will not produce any legal effects until clearance is granted.	The Act does not apply to public services concessionaires within the scope of the concession contract. Merger control provisions do not apply to the banking, financial or insurance sectors, which are, nevertheless subject to special provisions of a prudential nature. Among other regulations, the Commercial Companies Code, financial and securities legislation, as well as foreign investment rules, may be relevant.
Republic of Korea					
Mandatory system.	Filing required within 30 days from the date of the underlying transactions.	30 days (may be extended by up to 60 days). Suspension effects: there is a 30 day waiting period following notification before the proposed merger/acquisition can be completed (may be shortened or extended).	The substantive test is whether or not a proposed merger/acquisition has an anti competitive effect upon the market. Market share is an important factor in determining whether there is such an effect.	Failure to file: fines of up to 100 million won. Implementation before clearance: the FTC may file an action for nullification of a merger against companies which are in violation of the suspension period; fines of up to 100 million won.	Special provisions relating to concentrations of *chaebol* (conglomerates) and to financial institutions.

Countries	Notification trigger/filing deadline	Clearance deadlines (Stage 1/Stage 2)	Substantive test for clearance	Penalties	Remarks
South Africa					
Mandatory system. Prescribed forms to be completed but limited detail required.	Notification must be made within seven days after the earlier of: the conclusion of the merger agreement, the public announcement of a proposed merger bid or the acquisition by a party of a controlling interest in another party.	With intermediate mergers the waiting period to obtain a certificate of clearance from the Commission is 30 days, subject to the right of the Commission to extend this period by no longer than 60 days. If no reply is received from the Commission in the prescribed period, approval is deemed to have been obtained. With large mergers the timing may be longer and no time is specified in which the Tribunal must conduct a hearing, save that it must be called within 15 days of being referred by the Commission to the Tribunal.	Whether the merger is likely to have the effect of preventing or lessening competition in a particular market. If so, are there technological, efficiency or other pro competitive gains which outweigh the anti competitive effect, and can the merger be justified on substantial public interest grounds?	An administrative fine of up to 10 per cent of South African turnover in and exports from South Africa may be imposed where parties implement a merger prior to obtaining approval or in breach of conditions set by the authorities. Provision is made for the authorities to order divestiture.	Social and political factors are relevant to the assessment of a proposed merger, in addition to ordinary issues of economic efficiency and consumer welfare. Special rules for foreign investments in banking and broadcasting.
Taiwan Province of China					
Mandatory system. Form of notification: special form.	All sizeable combinations of entities in Taiwan Province of China where: (i) the surviving enterprise will acquire a market share reaching 1/3; or (ii) a participating enterprise holds a market share reaching 1/4; or (iii) the sales of a participating enterprise exceed NT$ 5 billion. Filing in advance of implementation.	The FTC must make its decision on clearance within two months after either receipt of an application or, if any amendment or supplement to the application is required, after receipt of such amendment or supplement. Suspension until clearance.	Whether the advantages of a combination to the overall economy of Taiwan outweigh the disadvantages resulting from the detriment to competition.	Failure to file; the FTC may (i) prohibit the combination; (ii) order separation of the combined enterprise; (iii) order disposal of all or part of the assets of the business; (iv) order discharge of personnel from their duties; (v) issue any other necessary order. Failure to file is also subject to an administrative fine of between NT$ 100 000 and 1 million, which may be assessed consecutively. Failure to comply with an FTC order may lead to a compulsory suspension, cessation or dissolution of business.	Special rules for foreign investments in telecom, financial services, etc.

Countries	Notification trigger/filing deadline	Clearance deadlines (Stage 1/Stage 2)	Substantive test for clearance	Penalties	Remarks
United States					
Mandatory system. Each party must submit a filing. Filing fee (paid by acquiring person) is US$ 45 000.	Must satisfy the commerce test, size of parties test and size of transaction test, and not qualify for an exemption. No filing deadline.	30 day initial waiting period (15 days for all cash tender offer). Can be extended or shortened by issuance of a Second Request. Stage 2 period ends on the 20th day after compliance by all parties with the Second Request (in the case of a cash tender offer, Stage 2 ends on the 10th day after compliance by the acquiring person with Second Request). Transaction suspended until waiting periods have been observed.	Whether the transaction may substantially reduce competition or tend to create a monopoly.	Failure to file: fine of up US$ 11 000 per day; divestiture can be required. Transaction cannot be implemented prior to clearance. Same penalties apply if transaction is consummated before approval.	Special rules can apply to certain industrial sectors (telecommunications, banking).
France					
Mandatory system	Pre-notification of concentration operations is mandatory if the statutory control thresholds, defined by the turnover of the enterprises concerned, are reached (total turnover above 150 million euros and individual turnover by at least two of the enterprises concerned in France exceeding 15 million euros). The parties can file at any time after they have reached an irrevocable commitment.	Stage 1 takes five weeks as from reception of the complete notification file (or up to a total of eight weeks if the parties submit late commitments). Stage 2, where the Competition Council is called upon to render an advisory opinion to the Minister, takes an additional four months (extendable for four more weeks if the parties submit late commitments). The operation is suspended until the final decision is made, except in the case of public bids (the shares may be acquired, without the rights being exercisable) or if a specific derogation has been granted to the parties having requested one.	The Minister verifies whether the operation "affects competition, in particular by creating or strengthening a dominant position or by creating or strengthening a purchasing power that places the suppliers in a situation of economic dependence", and possibly whether the operation makes "a sufficient contribution to economic and social progress to offset the effects on competition". The parties can propose commitments such as to remedy the problem of competition. At the end of Stage 2, the Minister can also issue injunctions subject to which the operation is authorized.	Failure to notify, or implementation before clearance: fine of up to five per cent of the turnover within France (1.5 million euros for natural persons). Omission or incorrect declaration in the notification: same fine and possible withdrawal of the authorization if granted, with the obligation to re-notify or re-establish the status quo ante. Failure to implement commitments or injunctions: referral of the case for an opinion from the Competition Council, which notes any non-compliance and fixes the sanction within the same limits; the Minister can also withdraw the authorization or prescribe a mandatory period for compliance.	The definition of the meaning of concentration and the method of calculating the turnover determining the obligation to notify are identical to those established by Commission Regulation 4064/89 in order to facilitate the task of enterprises when seeking to determine the control to which they are subject. There are special provisions for the audio-visual media and the banking sector. Operations having a minor impact on the markets in question are covered by a simplified notification file (case of no market affected).

2. Countries with mandatory postclosing notification system

Countries	Notification trigger/filing deadline	Clearance deadlines (Stage 1/Stage 2)	Substantive test for clearance	Penalties	Remarks
Argentina					
Mandatory system.	Mergers and acquisitions of companies with sales in Argentina equal to or in excess of US$ 200 million or worldwide revenues exceeding US$ 2.5 billion are subject to prior approval. Filing: prior to or within a week of execution of the agreement, publication of bid or acquisition of control.	45 days.	Whether the merger or acquisition would create or consolidate a dominant position on the market from which a detriment to the general economic interest might result.	Failure to file subject to a penalty of up to US$ 1 million per day of delay. Penalties for concluding a merger or acquisition in violation of the law may give rise to penalties of between US$ 10 000 and US$ 150 million. The courts could also order the dissolution, winding up, deconcentration or spin off of the companies involved.	There is no practical experience of the application of the law which has just been enacted. The implementing regulations to be dictated should clarify some provisions of the law.
Japan					
Mandatory system. Form of notification: filing of formal report to the Fair Trade Commission (FTC). Notification must be submitted in Japanese.	Amendments to the law, which became effective on 1 January 1999, have relaxed the requirements for merger and business transfer filings by establishing monetary thresholds. Under these amendments, only mergers and business transfers between a company having total assets of more than ¥ 10 billion and a company having total assets of more than ¥ 1 billion will be subject to a filing requirement.	No company shall consummate a merger or business transfer until after the expiration of a 30 day waiting period, which runs from the date that the FTC formally accepts the merger or business transfer notification, in the absence of any objection from the FTC.	Clearance will be given if the merger's or business transfer's effect does not substantially restrain competition in the relevant market.	Failure to file: maximum fine of ¥ 2 million. Implementation before clearance: maximum fine of ¥ 2 million.	A revenue threshold applies to the acquisition of a new Japanese company.
Spain					
Mandatory system. Form of notification: special form. Detailed information similar to Form CO. In Spanish.	Combined turnover in Spain over Ptas 40 billion and at least two parties over Ptas 10 billion each or combined market share in Spain (or in a "defined" market within Spain) of 25 per cent or more. Filing prior to completion and in any case within one month following signing of the agreement.	Stage 1: one month from notification. Stage 2: seven months from notification.Suspension: no suspensory obligation.	Whether the merger will affect the Spanish market, in particular through the creation or strengthening of a dominant position which impedes the maintenance of effective competition.	Failure to file: fines up to Ptas 5 million. Failure to notify after having been requested to file by the authorities: fines up to Ptas 2 million per day of delay. Implementation before clearance: no penalties.	Special provisions in the electricity, banking, telecom and insurance sectors.

3. Countries with voluntary notification system

Countries	Notification trigger/filing deadline	Clearance deadlines (Stage 1/Stage 2)	Substantive test for clearance	Penalties	Remarks
New Zealand					
A voluntary system applies for all mergers that would or would be likely to result in dominance acquired or strengthened (guidelines). Form of notification: special form.	Applies to all mergers. Would or would be likely to result in dominance being acquired or strengthened (guidelines). No formal time limit. Consent, if required, must be sought and obtained prior to closure.	No formal timetable applies. Clearance process: 10 business days. Authorization process: 60 business days. May be extended if agreed to by applicants. Suspension effects: closure cannot be effected without approval.	The merger or acquisition must not result, or be likely to result, in the acquiring or strengthening of a dominant position in a market. The Act does permit the above, however, if the detriment to competition is offset by benefit to the public.	No penalties for failure to file and/ or implementation before clearance. Contravention of the Act may result in a range of orders and penalties, including injunction, fines up to NZ$ 5 million (US$ 2.25 million), orders as to divestment and management, and damages.	Foreign investment in New Zealand is subject to foreign investment approval requirements (particularly if the acquisition involves land). Mergers and acquisitions may also need to comply with the companies Act, Overseas Investment Act and the Stock Exchange Listing Rules.
Norway					
Voluntary system. There are no jurisdictional thresholds. The Competition Authority may intervene in a merger up to six months from the date of the final agreement.	There are no jurisdictional thresholds (but non binding guidelines). No deadlines for filing.	The Competition Authority may intervene in a merger up to six months from the date of the final agreement (may be extended to one year). A voluntary filing starts an opposition procedure under which the Competition Authority has three months to decide whether or not it will investigate the merger further. If the Authority does not react within the three month period, the transaction is considered cleared. If it decides to investigate it has six months to decide. Implementation is not suspended during the investigation by the competition Authority.	The substantive test for clearance is whether the transaction will create or strengthen a significant restriction of competition. The substantive test for clearance consists of three stages: (1) Whether the combined market share of the parties exceeds 40 per cent, or the market shares of the three largest market players, including the parties, exceed 60 per cent; (2) Whether the parties as a result of the transaction will be able to exercise market power; (3) Whether the transaction will create efficiency gains that will outweigh the negative effects of the restriction of competition.	There are no fines or other penalties for not notifying a transaction, or for implementing a transaction prior to a clearance from the Competition Authority. Non compliance with decisions of the Competition Authority is a criminal offence and may lead to fines or imprisonment of up to three years (six years in aggravated circumstances). The Competition Authority may also impose periodic penalty payments, and require the parties to relinquish all gains derived as a result of non compliance with decisions of the Competition Authority.	Special rules for banking, insurance, shipping, mining, power, media, telecoms, and for agriculture. Mandatory notification requirement under the Acquisition Act 1994.

Countries	Notification trigger/filing deadline	Clearance deadlines (Stage 1/Stage 2)	Substantive test for clearance	Penalties	Remarks
United Kingdom					
Voluntary system. Form of notification: formal or informal. If formal, OFT's prescribed form. In English.	UK turnover of target over £70 million or combined market share in UK of 25 per cent created or enhanced. Filing, no formal time limit.	No formal timetable unless formal notification made Stage 1: usually four to seven weeks. Stage 2: maximum of 24 weeks in principle, although extensions are possible. Suspension effects: no suspension effects.	Whether the merger will be expected to result in a substantial lessening of competition.	Failure to file: no penalties. Implementation before clearance: no penalties.	Special provisions for media, water companies. National security can be used as a factor in decisions.
Venezuela					
Voluntary system. Form of notification: special form.	Aggregate amount of sales exceeds the equivalent of US$ 1.8 million. There are no filing deadlines.	Four months. May be extended by a further two months. Suspension effects: none.	Factors to be considered: (1) level of concentration in the relevant market before and after the transaction; (2) barriers to entry for new competitors; (3) availability of substitutable products; (4) possibility of collusion between the remaining suppliers; and (5) efficiencies of the transaction (effective competition, interests of consumers, promotion of cost reduction and development of new technology).	There are no penalties for not filing, or for consummating the transaction before clearance.	Special rules for the calculation of thresholds for banks and insurance companies. Special rules for insurance and telecom sectors. If a transaction is not notified, Procompetencia may open a proceeding to investigate the impact of the transaction on competition in the Venezuelan market within one year following the consummation of the transaction.

DATE DUE

Demco, Inc. 38-293